TOP-UP
LISTENING

Bill Holden, Chris Cleary, Terry Cooney

Series Editor: Maurice Jamall

2

ABAX

Series Editor: Maurice Jamall
Project Manager: Alastair Graham-Marr
Syllabus Design: Maurice Jamall / Alastair Graham-Marr

Editing and Proofing:
Maurice Jamall
Alastair Graham-Marr
Hugh Graham-Marr

Lexical Analysis: Rob Waring
Interactive Word List devised by Maurice Jamall
Compilation of Word Lists: Hugh Graham-Marr

Published by ABAX Ltd.,
Tokyo and San Francisco

Editorial Office • Tel: +81(0)-44-813-2909 / Fax +81(0)-44-813-2916

email • sales@abax.co.jp

homepage • www.abax.net

Layout and Cover Design by Design Office TERRA
Illustrations by Glen Giron, Ibarra Crisostomo and Leo Cultura of
Raketshop, Philippines.
Many thanks to Tina Ferrato, Guy Modica, Junko Saito
and David Moran for help in checking the scripts.

ISBN 1-896942-14-8

Inside *Top-Up Listening*

Top-Up Listening is a three-book skills-based series designed to help elementary to low-intermediate level students of English improve their listening abilities. The series gives students the chance to hear English as it is naturally used, in a wide variety of contexts including formal and informal conversations, announcements, telephone talk, and much, much more. In other words, *Top-Up Listening* provides students with the opportunity to develop their listening skills in the wide range of situations that they may well meet in the real world.

Organization

Each book in the *Top-Up Listening* series consists of 15 units built around topics and themes selected for their appropriacy to teenagers and young adults. Each unit is designed to take between 50 and 70 classroom minutes. At the back of the book students are provided with the scripts of the listening tasks and a glossary* of useful words and expressions. There is also space for students to include words they choose themselves.

Listening Task Types

The listening activities in *Top-Up Listening* are designed to develop different kinds of skills including listening for main points, for general understanding, for specific information and inferencing. Each unit has a main listening task which forms the basis of the unit. Some listenings are longer and introduce students to extensive listening. Other listenings are shorter and develop students' intensive listening abilities. The language in the listenings is graded to meet the level of the students, but naturally occurring features of spoken English are retained to give students listening material which realistically simulates authentic speech and is at the same time challenging but within reach. An American English model is used but other forms of native speaker English have also been included to introduce and expose students to the different types of English they will encounter outside the classroom.

Listening Clinic

A key focus in *Top-Up Listening* is the *Listening Clinics*. These are short, intensive listening tasks which highlight high-frequency phonological points. Students' difficulties understanding spoken English often come from an inability to decode a stream of connected speech. In each *Listening Clinic*, students focus on a single aspect of pronunciation.** Focusing intensively on these high-frequency features helps students grow more comfortable with English as it is spoken in the real world.

* The glossary is interactive requiring students to provide their own definitions or translations as well as locate items from definitions. By doing this students consolidate and review their work more thoroughly.

** This includes weak forms, liaison, assimilation and intonation and its uses. We have devised a set of terms to describe phonology which demystifies and simplifies so that the students are not put off by technical jargon.

Understanding Spoken English

Spoken English is very different from written English. When words are written down, there are spaces between them showing where one ends and the next word begins. For example, we write: "Would you like a sandwich?" But when we speak, there are no clear spaces, so we say:

"wouldyoulikeasandwich?"

To make things more difficult, sounds in words often mix or are lost, and so we say:

"wujewlaikasanwich?"

Top-Up Listening explains how English is spoken in the sections called *Listening Clinics*. Here you learn how to recognize the way people speak English and use this information to help you better understand what is being said and get to the speaker's meaning quicker. Here are some of the key points covered in the *Listening Clinics*:

1. Lost Sounds: In naturally spoken English, sounds are sometimes lost altogether.
   Example: *He's a postman.* The *t* sound is lost, so we hear: *He's a posman.*

2. Joined Sounds: When words end with a consonant and the following word begins with a vowel, the consonant 'jumps over' so that speech is smooth:
   Example: *He's an artist.* When spoken, it sounds like: *He sa nartist.*

3. Helping Sounds: When two vowels are next to each other, a "helping sound" often comes between them to make speaking easier. There are three helping sounds: *y*, *w*, and *r*.
   Examples: *y*: *She isn't here.* This becomes: *She-y-isn't here.*
   w: *I'd like to open the window.* This becomes: *I'd like to-w-open...*
   r: *America and Canada.* this becomes: *America-r-and Canada.*

4. Changing Sounds: Sounds can change from the spelling in spoken English.
   Examples: *He lives in Belgium.* The *n* becomes an *m* sound, so what you hear is: *He lives im Belgium.*
   I like football. The *b* changes to a *p* (the *t* is lost), and so what you hear is: *I like foopall.*

5. Weak Forms: The schwa (the upside-down *e* in the pronunciation alphabet) is the most common sound in English. Vowels are often spoken weakly. Say *Canada* and then say *Japan.* The first *a* sound in each country is different. In Canada the first *a* is strong and in Japan it is weak.

We hope you find using *Top-Up Listening* to be an enjoyable and rewarding experience.

In Your Own Time

Each unit in this textbook ends with a section called *In Your Own Time*. Here we ask you to work alone after the lesson so that you can review the things you did in class. If you spend some time each week reviewing what you study in class, you will make faster progress with your English.

At the back of your textbook, you will find the following:

- the scripts for all the listening exercises (pages 83 to 103).
- word lists with words and expressions from each unit (pages 105 to 113).
- your own copy of the CD that your teacher uses in the class.

Look at the back of the book now. Find the word lists, scripts and your CD.

Here are a few ways to use your textbook on your own.

Build Your Vocabulary

In each unit, you will see new words. In the word list you will find nine words and definitions. Some of the information is missing. You can complete the missing information by going through the unit again and reading through the scripts. If you want to, use a bilingual dictionary. If it helps you remember the word, write a translation in your own language. There is also space at the end of the word list for you to choose three new words for yourself. Try to choose words which you think are especially useful. Perhaps during the lesson, the teacher taught you some extra words and expressions not in the textbook. If you want to, you could write some of those words here. Don't add too many new words though. A good rule is to try to learn between eight and twelve new words per unit.

Work On Your Listening

During the lesson, your teacher has to teach the class at a speed that is comfortable for the most students. Sometimes the lessons may be too fast for you. Sometimes the lesson may go too slowly. But when you use your CD at home, you can always go at just the right speed for you. Here are some ways to make the most of your textbook to improve your listening:

- look at your answers to the listening tasks and listen to the recordings again.
- read through the scripts and check any new words and expressions, then close your book and listen to the recording(s) once more.
- read the script and listen to the CD at the same time.
- listen to the two *Listening Clinics* and then read them aloud.

One last piece of advice: don't do too much at one time. A good rule is *a little and often*. Just as we eat three times a day, it is much better to study for 15 or 20 minutes every day rather than for a long time just once a week.

By making the most of your textbook, you will really start to make progress with your English. Good luck with your studies.

Top-Up 2 Contents

It's famous for soccer

Let's Start!

Work in a group of three. Ask and answer the questions.

What are some famous places in your country?

What are some famous places in your city?

What is your country famous for?

What is your city famous for?

Work with your partner. Look at the maps. Write the name of the country under the picture. Choose from the countries in the box.

....

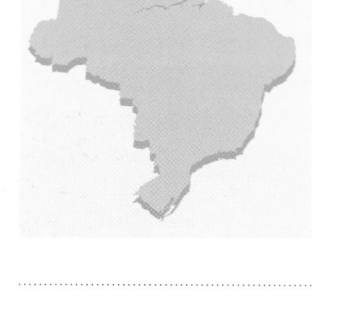

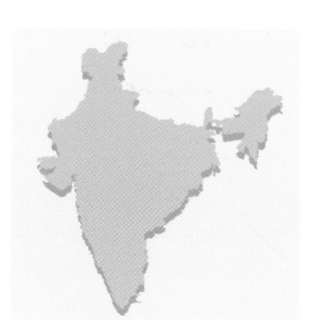

....

■ Brazil	■ France	■ Egypt	■ the UK
■ Japan	■ India	■ Spain	■ the US
■ Indonesia	■ Italy	■ Chile	■ Sweden

Check your answers with your teacher.

▸ Words

Work with your partner. Match the words to the pictures.

island
countryside
festival
parade
sightseeing
beaches
mountains

▸ Before You Listen

Work in a group of three. Use the information below to make sentences about these countries. e.g. ***France is famous for fashion.***

Brazil		cars
France		fashion
Egypt	is good at (*mak*ing)	movies
the UK		food
Japan		business
India	is famous for	cameras
		soccer
		music
		wines
		beaches
		coffee

Compare your sentences with other groups. Who has the most sentences?

▶ Let's Listen!

Listen to someone describing six countries. Write the number of the description next to the country.

...... India   ...... Egypt   ...... the UK

...... Japan   ...... France   ...... Brazil

Check your answers with your partner.

▶ Listen Again

Listen to the descriptions again. Place a check (✓) if the topic is mentioned in the description of the country.

	Cars	Island	Music	History	Festivals	Food	Fashion
Description 1	☐	☐	☐	☐	☐	☐	☐
Description 2	☐	☐	☐	☐	☐	☐	☐
Description 3	☐	☐	☐	☐	☐	☐	☐
Description 4	☐	☐	☐	☐	☐	☐	☐
Description 5	☐	☐	☐	☐	☐	☐	☐
Description 6	☐	☐	☐	☐	☐	☐	☐

Check your answers with your partner.

Which two countries would you most like to visit? Why?

▶ Listening Clinic One: Weak Vowels

Sometimes vowels are pronounced more weakly than others.

Example Have you ever been to America? → Have yo/u ever been to /America?

Listen to the dialogue. Draw a slash (/) through vowels that are pronounced *weakly*.

A: I want to go to Thailand.
B: Really? Why?
A: They've got great beaches and spicy cooking and beautiful temples.
B: And things are not expensive, right?
A: Right.
B: And the nightlife's fantastic.
A: Yeah, I've heard.
B: Can I come too?

Check your answers with your partner. Now say the dialogue together.

Practice!

Work with your partner. Follow the prompts and play the guessing game. Take turns to be Student A and Student B. Describe three countries each.

Student A:

Think of a country you know well and three things it is famous for.

Student B:

Listen to your partner. Ask questions. Try to guess the country.

Student A

Tell your partner what part of the world (Africa, Asia, the Americas…) it's in

e.g. *It's in Europe.*

Answer B's question(s)

Student B

Ask what the country is famous for

Tell your partner your guess

Now Listen Back

Listen to the descriptions again. Circle *Yes* or *No* to answer the first question. Write the answer to the second.

Does the speaker tell you anything about the people of the country? If *Yes*, what does he say?

Description 1	Yes	No	....
Description 2	Yes	No	....
Description 3	Yes	No	....
Description 4	Yes	No	....
Description 5	Yes	No	....
Description 6	Yes	No	....

Check your answers with your partner.

Work with your partner. Look at the sentences. Draw a slash (/) through any vowels which may be *spoken weakly*.

1. It's famous for beautiful beaches.
2. There's a huge festival every year.
3. Cafes are part of the popular culture.
4. There's an international film festival.
5. It's famous for international business.
6. It's between Mexico and Canada.

Listen and check. Now say the sentences.

⏵ Try It Out!

Work in two groups, Group A and Group B.

Group A: You are planning a one-week overseas vacation. Write down two or three things you want to see, to do, to eat and to shop for on your holiday. Then ask a travel agent for advice about where to go, what to see, what to do, what to eat, what to shop for.

The night life is great.

It has lovely old buildings.

It's famous for the night market.

A really relaxing holiday.

Group B: You are travel agents. Look at the information about the countries in this unit. Listen to your customer's ideas (students from Group A). Use the information in this unit to recommend a country for them to visit or recommend another country you know.

Find a partner from the other group and roleplay your conversation. Speak to three different students.

⏵ In Your Own Time

**Turn to page 105 and complete the word list. Use your dictionary if you want to.
Use the CD at the back of your book and listen to the recordings in this unit again. The script for this unit is on page 83.**

Unit 2 — How have you been?

⊹ Let's Start!

Work with your partner. Ask and answer the questions.

■ What are some common greetings in your language?
■ Do you use different greetings in the morning, afternoon and evening?
■ How many greetings do you know in English?

Work with your partner. Look at the greetings. Circle the language it comes from. The first one is done for you.

Greeting	Language	
Bonjourno	(Italian)	Spanish
Buenos dias	Italian	Spanish
Konnichiwa	Japanese	Korean
Ahn-young hah-say-oh	Japanese	Korean
Guten Tag	French	German
Comment ca va?	French	German

Check your answers with another pair.

Do you know any greetings from other languages?

⊹ Before You Listen

Work with your partner. Draw lines to match the things on the left you say when you meet people with the replies on the right. The first one is done for you. There may be more than one answer.

Greetings	Replies
What's up? ●	● Fine, thanks.
It's been a while, hasn't it? ●	● Not much.
How's it going? ●	● It sure has.
How have you been? ●	● Yeah, so what's new?
Sorry I'm late. ●	● Nice to see you, too.
It was nice to see you. ●	● Ah, that's okay.
Long time, no see. ●	● Fine, thanks, and yourself?

Which of these greetings can be formal? Which are usually casual?

Listen to four conversations. Check (✓) the boxes to complete the sentences.

Conversation 1

The speakers are…	☐ students.	☐ friends.	☐ business people.
They are in…	☐ a classroom.	☐ a cafeteria.	☐ an office building.
The number of people talking is…	☐ two.	☐ three.	☐ four.

Conversation 2

The speakers are…	☐ students.	☐ co-workers.	☐ business people.
They are in…	☐ the street.	☐ a bar.	☐ an office building.
The number of people talking is…	☐ two.	☐ three.	☐ four.

Conversation 3

The speakers are…	☐ friends.	☐ co-workers.	☐ relations.
They are in…	☐ a bar.	☐ a cafeteria.	☐ a restaurant.
The number of people talking is…	☐ two.	☐ three.	☐ four.

Conversation 4

| The speakers are in… | ☐ a bar. | ☐ a cafeteria. | ☐ the street. |
| The number of people talking is… | ☐ two. | ☐ three. | ☐ four. |

Check your answers with your partner.

Listen Again

Listen to the conversations again. Number the phrases in the order you hear them. The first one is done for you for each conversation.

Conversation 1

...... *How's it going?*   ..1.. *What's up?*   ...... *What's new?*

...... *Pretty good.*   ...... *Not bad.*   ...... *See you later.*

Conversation 2

...... *It's been a while, hasn't it?*   ...... *Glad to hear that.*   ...... *Sounds great.*

...... *Good seeing you.*   ...... *How about yourself?*   ..1.. *How have you been?*

Conversation 3

...... *What's new?*   ...... *Long time no see.*   ...... *How have you been?*

..1.. *How are you doing?*   ...... *Pretty good.*   ...... *I can't complain.*

Conversation 4

...... *All the best then.*   ...... *Fine thanks.*   ..1.. *How are you?*

...... *Nice to see you again.*   ...... *It's wonderful to see you.*   ...... *It's been a while, hasn't it?*

Check your answers with your partner.

⊹ Listening Clinic One: Joined Sounds

When a word ends in a consonant and the next word starts with a vowel, the consonant jumps over and joins the vowel. This makes it easier to say.

Example She works in an old office. → She work si na nol doffice.

Listen to the dialogue. Circle places where sounds _join_. The first two are done for you.

A: Have you met anyone interesting this week?
B: I met a woman in the library.
A: Is she a student?
B: No, she works in a record store.
A: What's her name?
B: Kylie Reeves. She's from Australia.

Check your answers with your partner. Now say the dialogue together.

⊹ Practice!

Work with your partner. Look at the three situations. Use the information and have three conversations. Use some of the phrases below to help you start your conversations.

Situation 1   Student A: You have been very busy with exams.
                        Student B: You have been very busy at your part-time job.

Situation 2   Student A: You saw a great movie last night.
                        Student B: You went to see your favorite band in concert last night.

Situation 3   Student A: A girl/boy you like asked you on a date this morning.
                        Student B: You had a fight with your girl/boyfriend this morning.

- ■ What's up?
- ■ How have you been?
- ■ How are you doing?
- ■ What's new?
- ■ Hi, how are you doing?
- ■ It's been a while, hasn't it?
- ■ Long time, no see.
- ■ Sorry I'm late.

Listen to the conversations again. Circle your answer to the questions.

Conversation	1	2	3	4
■ Do all the people in the conversation meet often?	Yes No	Yes No	Yes No	Yes No
■ Will they meet again soon?	Yes No Don't know	Yes No Don't know	Yes No Don't know	Yes No Don't know
■ Is the conversation formal (*F*) or casual (*C*)?	F C	F C	F C	F C

Check your answers with your partner.

‣ Listening Clinic Two: Joined Sounds

Work with your partner. Look at the sentences. Circle the places where sounds may *join*.

1. We're in a couple of classes together.
2. She isn't here yet, is she?
3. I've got an appointment with an old friend.
4. I'd like you to meet an old friend of mine.
5. Can I get you a drink?
6. I'm here to meet a friend.

Listen and check. Now say the sentences.

⊡ Try It Out!

Work as a class. Walk around and greet some of the other students. Ask and answer questions about what you've been doing recently. Use the prompts to help you. Speak to at least four people.

A	B
Greet your partner ●	● Reply
Reply. Ask what your partner has been doing ●	● Reply. Ask the same question
Reply ●	● Show interest. Say it was nice to see A
Say it was nice to see B ●	● Say goodbye
Say goodbye ●	

⊡ In Your Own Time

Turn to pages 105 and 106 and complete the word list. Use your dictionary if you want to. Use the CD at the back of your book and listen to the recordings in this unit again. The script for this unit is on pages 84 and 85.

Can I help you ma'am?

⁙ Let's Start!

Look at the pictures. Write the name of each item under the picture. Choose from the words below.

....

....

■ cell phone   ■ television   ■ car navigator
■ camera   ■ computer/PC   ■ videogame console

Place a check (✓) next to the items that you have in your home. Place a cross (✗) next to *one* that you would like to buy.

Compare your answers with your partner.

⁞ Words

Work with your partner. Write the feature in the correct box/boxes. The first one is done for you.

Cell Phone	TV	Car Navigator	Computer	Videogame Console
memory		memory	memory	memory

- memory
- range
- screen
- channel
- map
- location
- touch-dial
- software
- dates
- email

Compare your answers with another pair.

⁞ Before You Listen

Work with your partner. Look at the following expressions. Circle S if the expression is usually used by the sales clerk. Circle C if the expression is usually used by the customer.

Expression

Can I help you?	S	C
I'm just looking, thanks.	S	C
Could you show me this one?	S	C
What price range are you thinking of?	S	C
How would you like to pay?	S	C
Can it get email?	S	C
How much is it?	S	C

Check your answers with another pair.

⊞ Let's Listen!

Listen to four conversations. Write the type of product that the customer and the sales clerk are talking about.

Conversation 1 ....   Conversation 3 ....

Conversation 2 ....   Conversation 4 ....

Check your answers with your partner.

⊞ Listen Again

Listen to Conversation 4 again. Check (✓) the points about each item.

	Sonic	Tote
stores lots of numbers	☐	☐
over $100	☐	☐
one-year warranty	☐	☐
heavy	☐	☐
light	☐	☐
free case	☐	☐
faster websurfing	☐	☐

Check your answers with your partner. Which of the two phones would you buy?

⊞ Listening Clinic One: Lost Sounds

Sometimes speakers don't pronounce all the sounds in the words. They are lost.

Example : How much is it? → How much is it? (The /t/ sound is lost)

Listen to the dialogue. Draw a line through the /t/ sounds which are *lost*.

A: What's the cheapest, simplest cell phone?
B: Buy a Tote. They're the best.
A: About how much does it cost to use?
B: Not that much. About sixty cents a day.
A: It's that cheap? That's great!
B: Yeah. It's a really good deal.

Check your answers with your partner. Now say the dialogue together.

⁚ Practice!

Work with your partner. Student A: You are a sales clerk. Student B: You are a customer. Practice the dialogue. Choose your own words where the ░░░ is. Take turns to be the sales clerk and the customer.

Sales Clerk: Good ░░░ sir/ma'am. May I help you?

Customer: Yes… I'm looking for a ░░░ .

Sales Clerk: Well. We have this one here, the ░░░ .

Customer: The ░░░ . Can it ░░░ ?

Sales Clerk: ⌈ Yes it can.
                 ⌊ I'm afraid it can't.

Customer: Uh huh. And how much does it cost?

Sales Clerk: It's ░░░ .

Customer: And does it come with a ░░░ ?

Sales Clerk: ⌈ Yes, it does.
                 ⌊ No, I'm afraid it doesn't.

Customer: ⌈ Great. I'll take it.
              ⌊ Hmm. Let me think about it.

⁚ Now Listen Back

Listen to the conversations again. Circle *Yes* if the customer is interested in the product. Circle *No* if the customer is not interested.

Conversation 1	Yes	No
Conversation 2	Yes	No
Conversation 3	Yes	No
Conversation 4	Yes	No

Check your answers with your partner.

⁚ Listening Clinic Two: Lost Sounds

Work with your partner. Look at the sentences. Draw a line through any /t/ sounds that may be *lost*.

1. It can send email, text messages and get information online.
2. It's also very light; you won't have to recharge it very often.
3. I see, but I'm a student and I can't buy anything like that.
4. Well, it sounds like what you want is a basic service.
5. Yes, but the best thing is you get the phone for free.
6. Just send the card that comes with it back to the company.

Listen and check. Now say the sentences.

▶Try It Out!

Work in four groups: A, B, C and D

Group A: You are sales staff.
You are selling computers.

Group B: You are sales staff.
You are selling cell phones.

Group C: You are sales staff.
You are selling videogame consoles.

Group D: You are customers.

Sales Staff: Think about your products: What can they do? How much do they cost?
How long is the warranty? Anything else?

Customers: Think of questions to ask the sales staff: *Does it...?*
Can it...?
How much...?
Do you have...?

Customers: Now visit the shops. Find out about the products. Do you want to buy any?

Sales Staff: Greet the customers. Tell them about your products. Can you sell any?

▶In Your Own Time

**Turn to page 106 and complete the word list. Use your dictionary if you want to.
Use the CD at the back of your book and listen to the recordings in this unit again. The
script for this unit is on pages 85, 86 and 87.**

Where's the toy department?

:Let's Start!

Work with your partner. Ask and answer the questions.

- Do you often buy presents for family and friends?
- What are the biggest department stores in your town?
- When did you last visit a department store?

:Words

Work with your partner. Look at the picture and the questions. Circle *Yes* or *No* to answer the questions.

Are the beachballs behind the water pistols?	Yes	No
Are the video games near the stairs?	Yes	No
Is the unicycle on the right of the dollhouse?	Yes	No
Are the yo-yos on the left of the playing cards?	Yes	No
Are the *Lego* sets in front of the hula hoops?	Yes	No
Are the letter blocks beside the ping pong table?	Yes	No
Is the rocking horse next to the scooters?	Yes	No
Are the crayons at the bottom of the bargain bin?	Yes	No

Expressions

Work with your partner. Write the number of the direction next to the correct phrase. The first one is done for you.

...... go toward the...
_1_ turn left
...... turn right
...... go past the...
...... walk straight
...... take the stairs

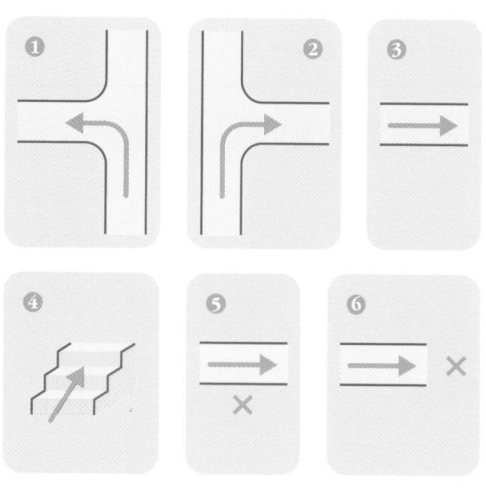

Before You Listen

Work with your partner. Draw lines to match the items on the left to their departments on the right.

Items	Department
skirts, blouses, dresses, slacks, coats ●	● Menswear
board games, skipping ropes, scooters ●	● Luggage
suits, trousers, neckties, jackets ●	● Home Entertainment
suitcases, handbags, purses, bags ●	● Toys
AV equipment, CDs, tapes, DVDs, cameras ●	● Ladieswear

Check your answers.

Let's Listen!

Listen to four conversations. Write the gift the customer wants to buy (if mentioned). Then write the floor number (if mentioned).

	Gift	Floor
Conversation 1	....	....
Conversation 2	....	....
Conversation 3	....	....
Conversation 4	....	....

Check your answers with your partner.

Listen to the conversations again. Draw the route the customer is told.

Conversation 1

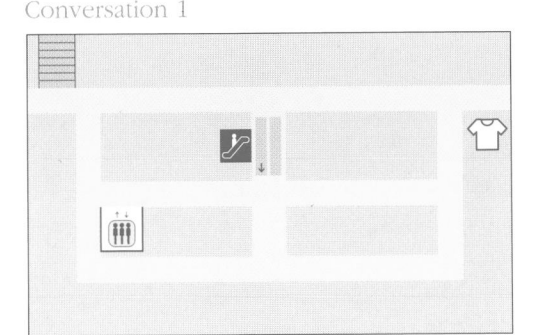

Conversation 2

Conversation 3

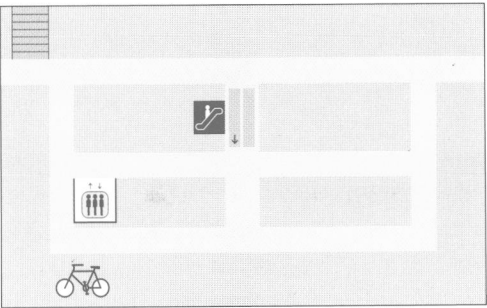

Conversation 4

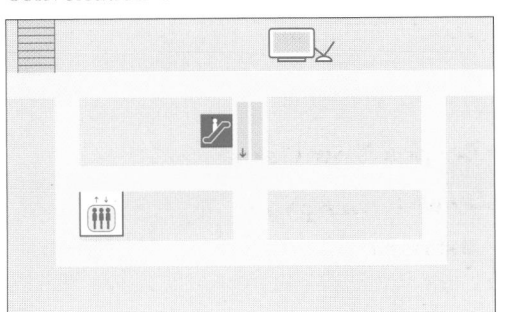

Check your answers with your partner.

⊱Listening Clinic One: Showing New Information

When the speaker wants to show that he is giving new information, the word which has the new information also has heavy stress.

> **Example** : I bought a shirt on Saturday. A <u>red</u> shirt. (*red* is new information)

Listen to the dialogue. Underline the words which have heavy stress to *show new information*. The first two are done for you.

A: I'd like to buy a <u>present</u> for my <u>wife</u>.
B: What kind of present?
A: Hmm. Maybe a scarf...
B: A scarf? Wool, silk or cotton?
A: Silk. She likes red.
B: A red silk scarf... let's see... How about this one?
A: That's nice.

Check your answers with your partner. Now say the dialogue together.

⋟Practice!

Work with your partner. Look at the floor plan. Follow the prompts and ask and give directions to different places in the store. Take turns to be the store clerk and the customer.

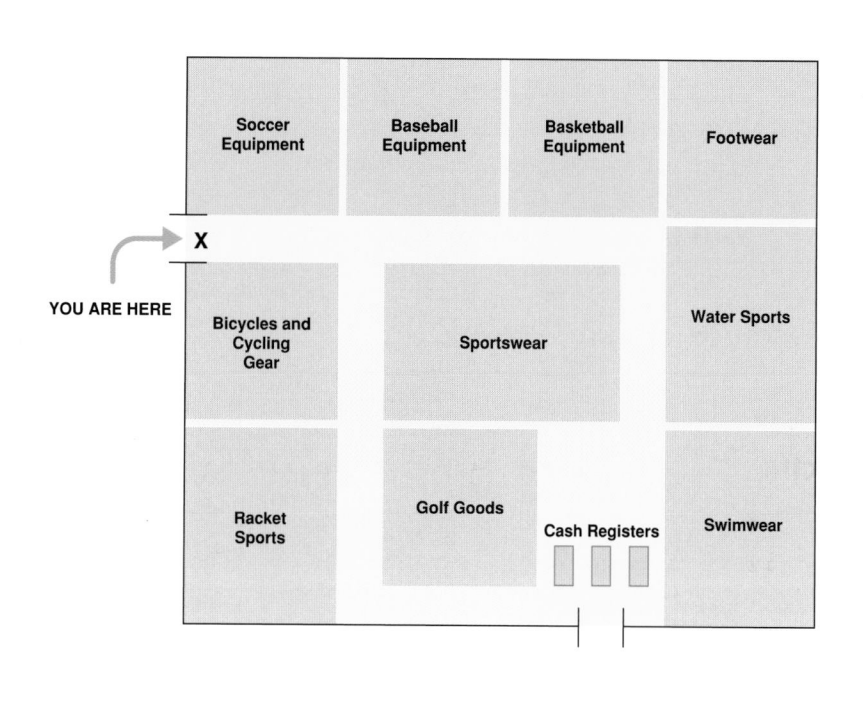

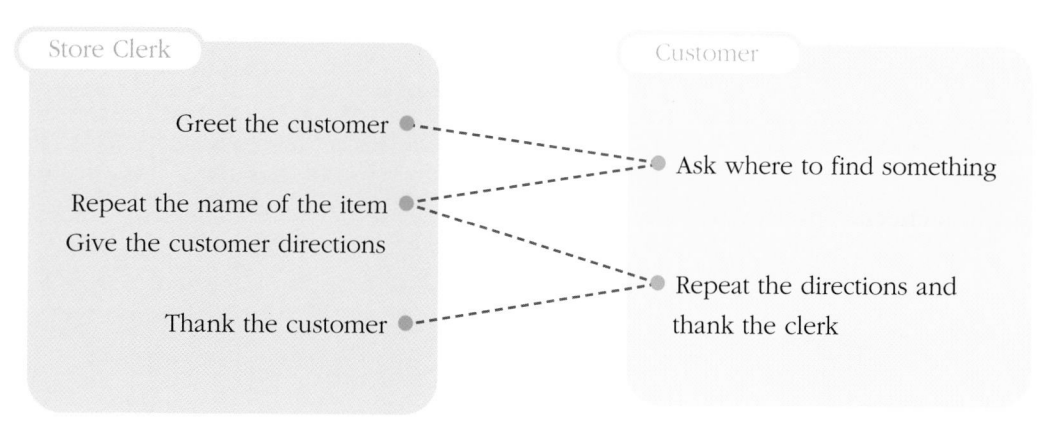

Listen to the conversations again. Answer the questions.

Conversation	1	2	3	4
Who is the gift for?	....	....	....	....
What gift idea(s) does the clerk suggest?	....	....	....	....
	....	....	....	....

Check your answers with your partner.

⊹Listening Clinic Two: Showing New Information

Work with your partner. Look at the dialogue. Underline words which may have heavy stress to *show new information*.

> A: Excuse me, where's the customer service counter?
> B: The service counter's in the back of the store, beside the elevator.
> A: In the back of the store, beside the elevator. Thanks. Can I exchange this there?
> B: Exchange what?
> A: This sweater. It was a gift, but it's too small.
> B: Too small. Why don't you go to Ladieswear?

Listen and check. Now say the dialogue together.

Work on your own. Look at the store plan below. Add the following departments to the store:

- Accessories
- Menswear
- Ladieswear
- Cosmetics
- Music
- Toys & Games
- Kitchenware
- Books
- Art Supplies

Now, look at the items below. Circle three that you would like to buy for friends or family members.

coffee maker	jeans	playing cards
paint set	purse	t-shirt
paperback	lipstick	CD

Work with your partner. Roleplay asking for directions in a department store. Student A: You are a clerk in the store. Student B: You are a customer looking for the three items you circled. Ask the clerk for directions.

Begin the roleplay like this: Clerk: *Can I help you?*   Customer: *Yes I'm looking for…*
Take turns to be the store clerk and the customer.

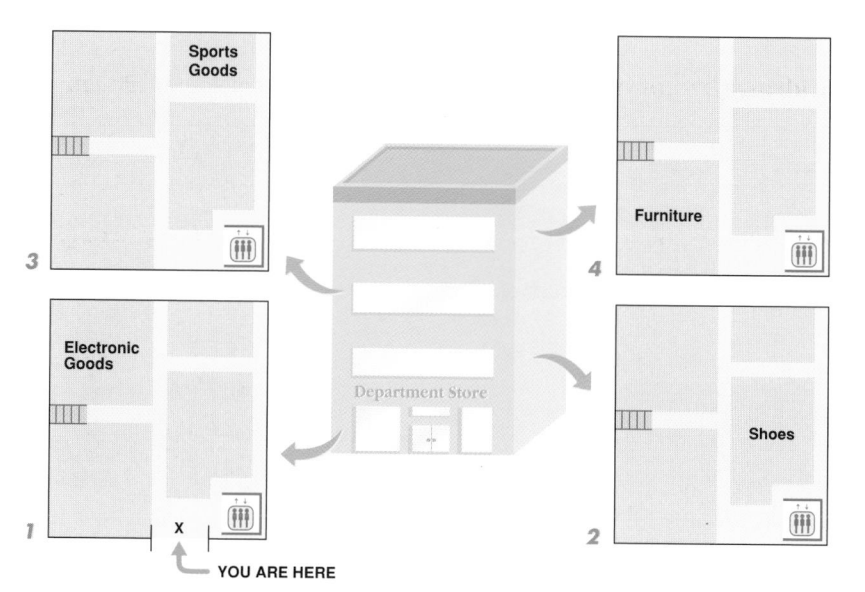

When you have both finished, look at your partner's store plan. Did you understand his/her directions correctly?

⋅In Your Own Time

Turn to pages 106 and 107 and complete the word list. Use your dictionary if you want to. Use the CD at the back of your book and listen to the recordings in this unit again. The script for this unit is on pages 87 and 88.

Unit 5 Two tickets for tonight's show

▶ Let's Start!

Work in a group of three. Ask and answer the questions.

- ■ Have you ever been to a concert? When did you last go?
- ■ What's the best concert you've ever been to?
- ■ What's the most famous concert hall in your area/city?

Work with your partner. Look at the table showing different kinds of concert. Place a check (✓) if you think the feature is connected with the kind of concert.

	Older people	Quite cheap	A large audience	Outdoors
Hip-Hop	☐	☐	☐	☐
Ballet	☐	☐	☐	☐
Classical	☐	☐	☐	☐
Rock/Pop	☐	☐	☐	☐
Jazz	☐	☐	☐	☐
Blues	☐	☐	☐	☐

Compare your ideas with another pair. Are they the same or a little different?

▶ Words

Work with your partner. Draw lines from the words to places in the picture.

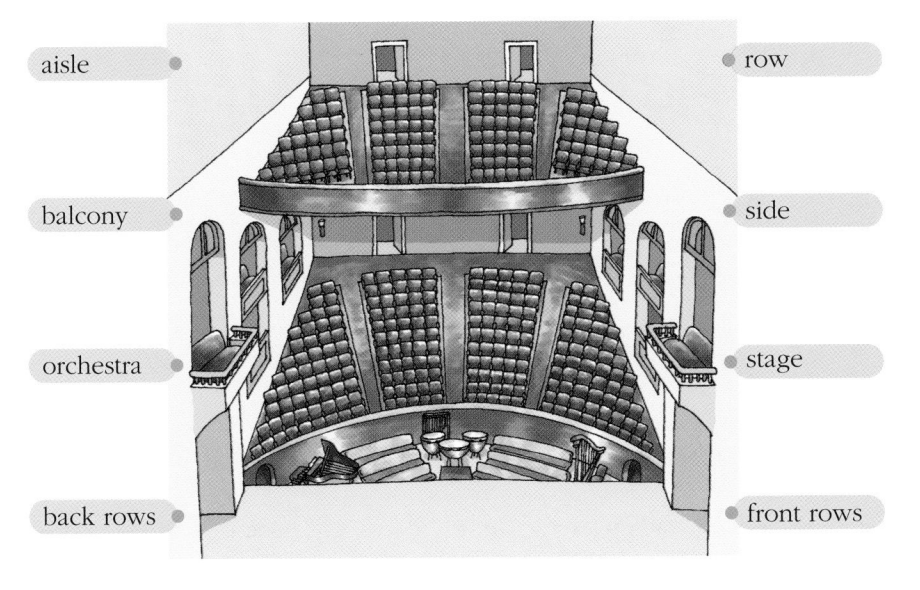

aisle
row
balcony
side
orchestra
stage
back rows
front rows

Check your answers with another pair.

Before You Listen

Work with your partner. Arrange the sentences to make a conversation between a caller and the clerk at a ticket office. The first one is done for you.

...... Fine. Can I pay by credit card?

...... Sorry, the show is sold out. There are no more tickets available.

...... Please hold, I'll just check. Yes sir. There's another show on Sunday.

...... $25, plus tax and service.

__1__ I'd like to reserve two tickets for Saturday's show, please.

...... Of course. Can I have your name, the card number and the expiry date?

...... Is there another performance?

...... Oh good. How much are the tickets?

Now say the dialogue with your partner.

Let's Listen!

Listen to four conversations. Circle *Yes*, *No* or *Don't Know* to answer the question.

Does the caller buy a ticket?

Conversation 1	Yes	No	Don't Know
Conversation 2	Yes	No	Don't Know
Conversation 3	Yes	No	Don't Know
Conversation 4	Yes	No	Don't Know

Check your answers with your partner.

Listen Again

Listen to Conversations 2, 3 and 4 again. Check (✓) the conversation in which you hear the information.

Conversation	2	3	4
Two tickets	☐	☐	☐
Four tickets	☐	☐	☐
April	☐	☐	☐
May	☐	☐	☐
June	☐	☐	☐
A few seats left	☐	☐	☐
Free seating	☐	☐	☐
Orchestra seats	☐	☐	☐
Stage-side seats	☐	☐	☐
$45.00	☐	☐	☐
$96.00	☐	☐	☐

Check your answers with your partner. Which concert would you like to go to?

⏵Listening Clinic One: Sounding Polite

When speakers want to show they are sounding polite, the pitch of the voice is higher.

Example	Could you please hold while I check on tickets? (polite pitching)
	Of course. (standard pitching)

Listen to the mini-dialogues. One speaker's voice is pitched higher than the other's to *sound polite* . Place a check (✓) in front of these sentences.

1. __ A: Yes, I'd like some ticket information, please.
    __ B: Of course. What event are you interested in?

2. __ A: I'm sorry to keep you waiting. I've reserved your tickets.
    __ B: Great. Can I pick them up at the box office?

3. __ A: Which concert are you interested in, sir?
    __ B: The *Jazz All Stars* concert in February.

4. __ A: Thank you very much. Will there be anything else?
    __ B: No, that'll be all.

Check your answers with your partner. Now say the dialogues together.

⏵Practice!

Work with your partner. Student A: You are a ticket agent. Student B: You are a customer. Practice the dialogue. Choose your own words where the ⬜ is. Take turns to be the ticket agent and the customer.

Ticket Agent: *Concert Choice.* May I help you?

Customer: Yes. I'd like ⬜ ticket(s) for the ⬜ concert on ⬜ .

Ticket Agent: ⬜ ticket(s) for the ⬜ concert on ⬜ ?

Customer: Yes.

Ticket Agent: One moment please… We have some ⬜ tickets left.

Customer: How much are those?

Ticket Agent: ⬜ each.

Customer: ⌈ Okay. I'll take one/them.
           ⌊ I see. Well thanks for your time.

⁞Now Listen Back

Listen to Conversations 2, 3 and 4 again. Circle the number of the conversation to answer the questions.

- Which customer is happiest with the seats?　　2　　3　　4
- Which customer is the hardest to satisfy?　　2　　3　　4

Check your answers with your partner.

⁞Listening Clinic Two: Sounding Polite

Work with your partner. Look at the dialogues. Place a check (✓) in front of the sentences which may be spoken in a higher voice to show the speaker is _sounding polite._

1.   __ A: May I help you?
       __ B: Yes, I'd like some information about a concert.

2.   __ A: I'll just check. Could you hold please?
       __ B: Of course.

3.   __ A: Can I use my MasterCard?
       __ B: Of course. Could I have your credit card number, please?

4.   __ A: I'd like four tickets for Saturday night's performance.
       __ B: I'm sorry. Was that this Saturday's performance, ma'am?

Listen and check. Now say the dialogues together.

⁞Try It Out!

Work with your partner. Student A: Turn to page 89. Student B: Turn to page 91.

⁞In Your Own Time

Turn to page 107 and complete the word list. Use your dictionary if you want to.
Use the CD at the back of your book and listen to the recordings in this unit again. The script for this unit is on pages 88 and 89.

Unit 6 — What can I get you?

Let's Start!

Work with your partner. Look at the pictures. Choose from the words on the left and write the name of each food under the picture.

- ■ Hot Dog
- ■ Hamburger
- ■ Sub
- ■ Pizza
- ■ Fried Chicken

Do you know a place near your school or home which sells each kind of food?

Class Survey

Look at the survey. Ask and answer these questions to three different students.

Survey Question	Partner 1	Partner 2	Partner 3
■ What's your favorite fast-food restaurant?			
■ How often do you go there?			
■ What food do you usually order there?			
■ Do you usually order a set meal or different things one by one?			
■ What restaurant do you dislike?			

Work with a new partner. Compare your information.

Work with your partner. Draw lines to match each phrase in Column A with a reply from Column B. The first one is done for your

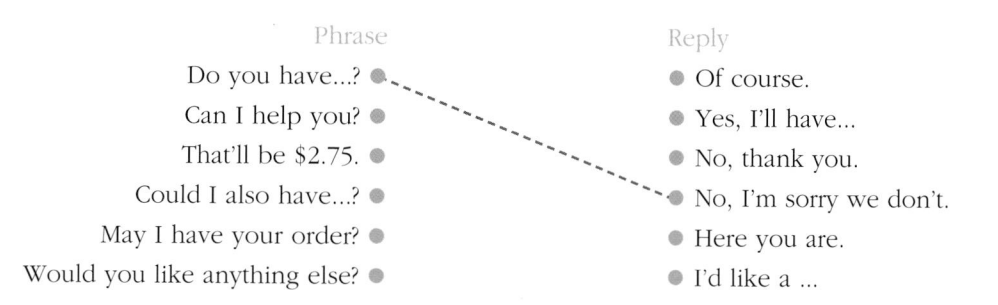

Phrase		Reply
Do you have...? ●	●	Of course.
Can I help you? ●	●	Yes, I'll have...
That'll be $2.75. ●	●	No, thank you.
Could I also have...? ●	●	No, I'm sorry we don't.
May I have your order? ●	●	Here you are.
Would you like anything else? ●	●	I'd like a ...

Work with your partner. Look at the pictures in *Let's Start!* again. Use some of the expressions and make up a conversation between a customer and counter staff in a fast food restaurant. Take turns to be the customer.

‡ **Let's Listen!**

Listen to three conversations. Look at the pictures. Write the number of the conversation next to the meal(s) that the customer orders.

:Listen Again

Listen to the conversations again. Circle your answer to the first question. Write your anwer to the second.

Does the customer take the food out or eat in the restaurant? How much does the food cost?

Conversation 1	Take out	Eat in	....
Conversation 2	Take out	Eat in	....
Conversation 3	Take out	Eat in	....

Compare your answers with your partner.

:Listening Clinic One: Mixed Sounds

Sometimes when two consonant sounds come together, one at the end of one word and one at the beginning of the next, they mix and make a new sound.

Example : Do you want something to drink? → Ju want something to drink?

Listen to the dialogue. Circle the places where you hear _mixed sounds_.

A: Would you like to order?
B: Can I have a deluxe cheeseburger set, fries and cola to go?
A: Did you want anything else with that?
B: Do you have any ice cream?
A: Do you want chocolate, vanilla or strawberry?
B: Chocolate. Could you give me some extra napkins?

Check your answers with your partner. Now say the dialogue together.

:Practice!

Work with your partner. Follow the prompts on the next page and practice giving and taking an order in a fast-food restaurant. Take turns to be the counter staff and the customer.

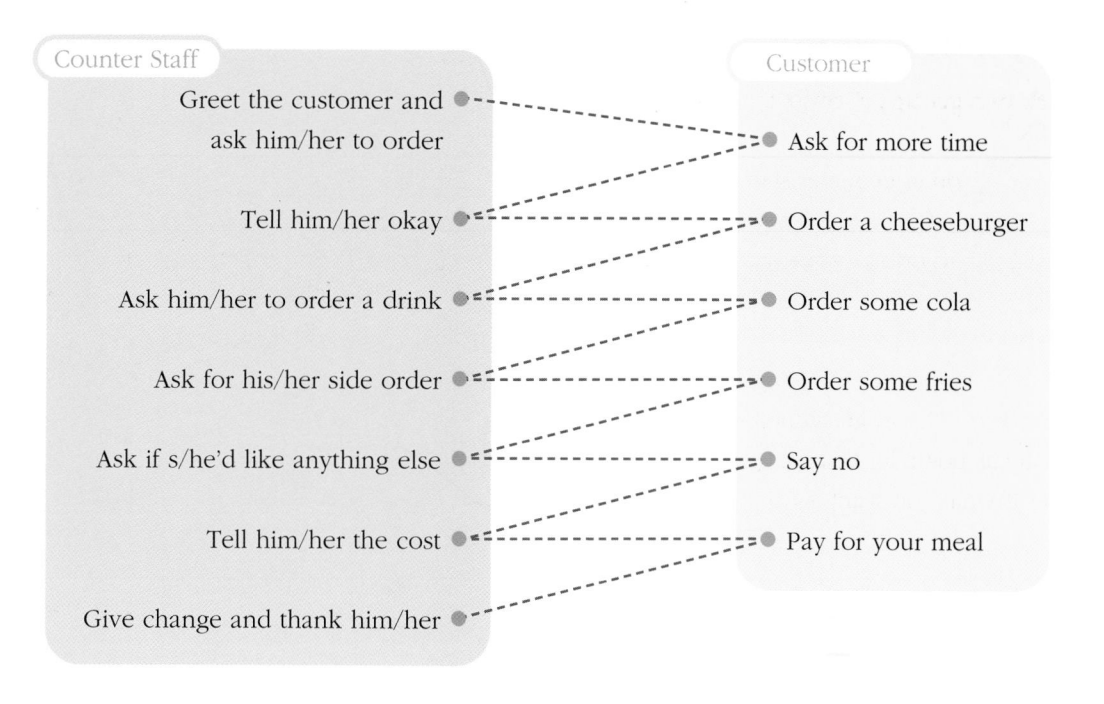

Now Listen Back

Listen to the conversations again. Draw lines from the conversation to the phrase(s) that is connected to it. You can draw more than one line.

- special food for children

Conversation 1 ●
- the woman at the counter quickly ends the conversation

Conversation 2 ●
- lots of drinks to choose from
- the customer wants more salt and pepper

Conversation 3 ●
- the customer wants lots of napkins
- the healthiest meal

Listening Clinic Two: Mixed Sounds

Work with your partner. Look at the sentences. Circle places where sounds may *mix*.

1. I'm sorry, could you give me a minute?
2. And would you like some fries to go with that shake?
3. And what did you want to drink?
4. You get a side dish. Do you want soup, salad or french fries?
5. What else would you like with that?
6. Did you want that for here or to go?

Listen and check. Now say the sentences.

Try It Out!

Work two groups, Group A and Group B.

Group A: You are counter staff. Look at the menu below. Circle five items. These five items are sold out. The customer cannot buy them.

Group B: You are customers. You are in a hurry. You want to get something to eat as quickly as possible. Be ready to change your order if what you want is not available.

You're welcome

I'm sorry, we don't have any left.

Thank you.

...and an apple tart, please.

Burgers of Babylon

Sandwiches

Hamburger	2.25
Doubleburger	2.75
Cheeseburger	2.40
Gardenburger	2.90
Babylon Deluxe	3.10
Salsa Burger	2.60
Fish Sandwich	2.60
Cajun Chickenburger	2.60
Veggieburger	2.40

Beverages

Cola	
Medium	1.25
Large	1.50
Jumbo	1.75
Babylon Shake	2.25
Coffee	0.75
Tea	0.75

Side Orders

Babylon Fries	
Medium	1.25
Large	1.75
Onion Rings	
Medium	1.75
Large	2.25
Garden Salad	2.25
Caesar Salad	2.75
Bean Soup	1.75

Desserts

Hot Apple Tart	1.75
Babylon Ice	2.25
Chocolate Malt	1.75

In Your Own Time

Turn to pages 107 and 108 and complete the word list. Use your dictionary if you want to. Use the CD at the back of your book and listen to the recordings in this unit again. The script for this unit is on pages 90 and 91.

I'm terribly sorry, sir

▸Let's Start!

Work in a group of three. Ask and answer the questions.

- How often do you eat in restaurants?
- Are there any restaurants near your school or home?
- Do you enjoy eating out?

Look at the problems that sometimes happen in restaurants. Circle the number to show how serious you think each problem is. Choose from *1* (not serious) to *4* (quite serious).

▪ slow service	1	2	3	4
▪ missing cutlery	1	2	3	4
▪ noisy customers nearby	1	2	3	4
▪ a mistake with your order	1	2	3	4
▪ a rude waiter	1	2	3	4
▪ badly prepared food	1	2	3	4
▪ a mistake on your check	1	2	3	4

Work with a partner from another group. Compare your answers.

Have you ever experienced any of these problems? What did you do?

▸Before You Listen

Work with your partner. Draw lines to match the phrases on the left with the correct ending on the right to make six sentences. The first one is done for you.

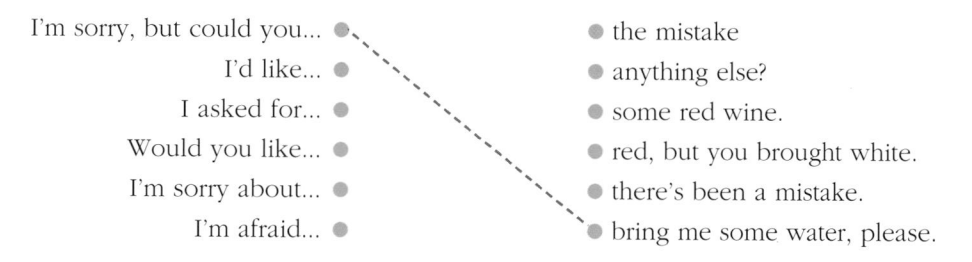

I'm sorry, but could you...
I'd like...
I asked for...
Would you like...
I'm sorry about...
I'm afraid...

the mistake
anything else?
some red wine.
red, but you brought white.
there's been a mistake.
bring me some water, please.

Now look at the three pictures. Which three sentences do they describe?

Look back at the six sentences. Which can be used to...

- ask for something
- offer something
- apologize
- complain

Let's Listen!

Listen to three conversations. Circle which type of meal they are having. Then draw lines to the problems they have.

	Meal			Problems
				● the cutlery is dirty
Conversation 1	[lunch	dinner] ●		● the food doesn't arrive
Conversation 2	[lunch	dinner] ●		● the drink is cold
Conversation 3	[lunch	dinner] ●		● the food is cold
				● the waiter gives the drink to the wrong person

Check your answer with your partner.

Listen Again

Listen to the conversation again. Write down the reason for the problem (if mentioned). Write down what the server offers to do.

	Reason for Problem (if mentioned)	Server offers to...
Conversation 1	....	....
Conversation 2	....	....
Conversation 3	....	....

Check your answer with your partner.

⊱Listening Clinic One: Contrasting Information

When a speaker wants to show that information is new or different from something said earlier, s/he puts stress on the word with the new information.

| **Example** | I'll have the chicken. What would <u>you</u> like? |

Listen to the dialogue. Underline the words which are stressed to *contrast* information.

A: Could I have a small Coke please?

B: I'm sorry, we don't have Coke. We have Pepsi, though.

A: Pepsi? In a bottle?

B: No, in a can. Do you want one?

A: Yeah, if that's all you have.

Check your answers with your partner.
Circle the stressed words that carry new information.
Now say the dialogue together.

⊱Practice!

Work in two groups.

Group A: You are waiters/waitresses. Look at the list of complaints.
What will you offer to do for the customer?

Group B: You are customers. Look at the list of problems.
Choose three to make. Decide what you want the waiter/waitress to do for you.

Customers

I'm sorry but...   *I didn't order this.*

this spoon is dirty.

I'm still waiting for a menu.

the people at the next table are smoking.

there's a mistake on the check.

that waiter was rude.

the coffee is cold.

Waiting Staff

I'm terribly sorry sir, I'll ... ?

Now work as a class. Waiters/waitresses: go around and listen to the complaints of different customers. Customers: complain to the waiters/waitresses.

Now go back to your group and discuss the following question.

Customers: who was the best waiter/waitress?

Waiting staff: who was the most difficult customer?

⋮Now Listen Back

Listen to the conversations again. Below is a list of relationships that people can have. Put a line through the two relationships that do *not* describe customers in the conversations.

business people   high school students   a family   old friends   delivery workers

Compare your answers with your partner.

⋮Listening Clinic Two: Contrasting Information

Work with your partner. Look at the sentences. Underline two words in each sentence which may be stressed to *contrast information*.

1. I ordered the chicken, he ordered the pasta.
2. I'm sorry, we don't have Coke. Is Pepsi alright?
3. Excuse me, this is the lunch menu. Could we see the dinner menu?
4. I'm afraid my glass is cracked. Could I have another one?
5. I'm sorry, this must be their order. I'll have yours in just a minute.
6. I asked for a fish knife. This is a butter knife.

Listen and check. Now say the sentences.

Work with your partner. Look at the picture and decide what is wrong. What will the customer say? What will the waiter/waitress say? Roleplay three of the situations. Take turns to be the customer and the waiter/waitress.

⊳In Your Own Time

Turn to page 108 and complete the word list. Use your dictionary if you want to.
Use the CD at the back of your book and listen to the recordings in this unit again. The script for this unit is on pages 92 and 93.

Now here's the weather

⊡ Let's Start!

Work with your partner. Ask and answer the questions.

- ▪ What's your favorite season? Why?
- ▪ What kind of weather do you like best?
- ▪ Is today's weather better than yesterday's?
- ▪ What are the hottest and coldest places you've ever visited?

Look at the map. Write the names of these regions on it.

- ▪ Northern Africa
- ▪ Northern Europe
- ▪ East Asia
- ▪ The Pacific
- ▪ Southern Africa
- ▪ Southern Europe
- ▪ The Middle East

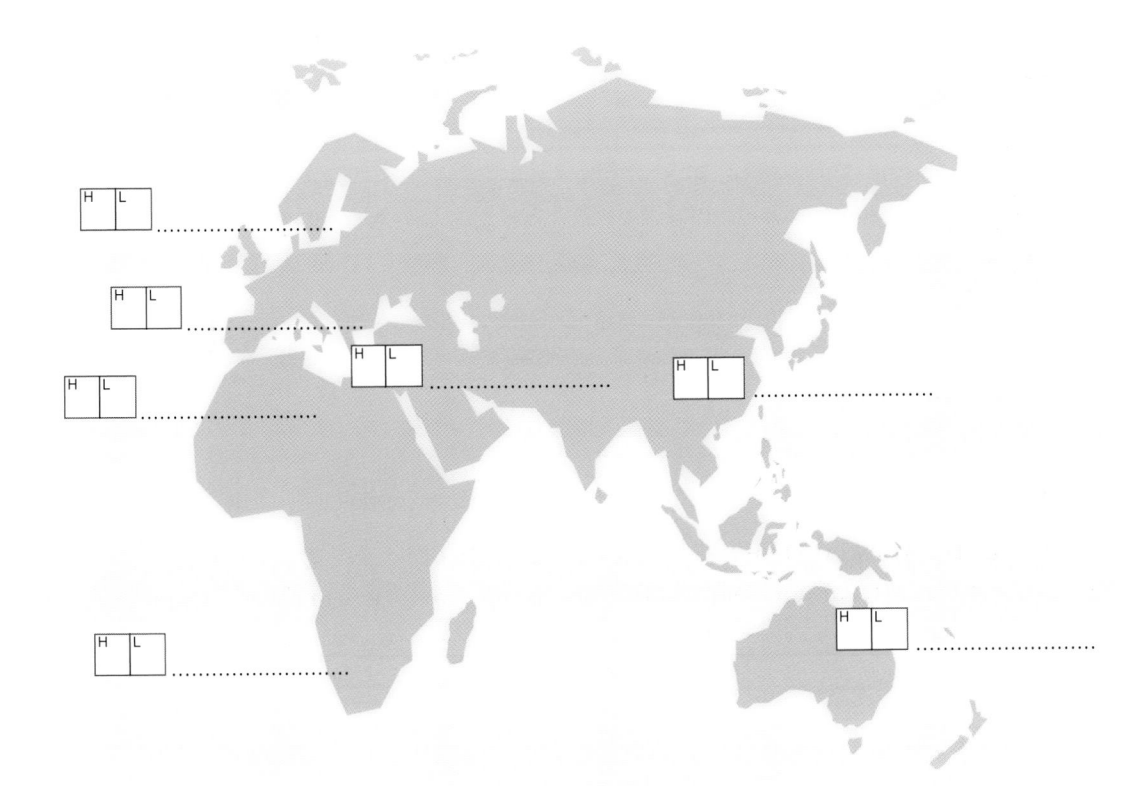

Which region do you think is hottest? Which do you think is coldest?

Words

Match the following words to the correct weather symbols. Write the letter of the symbol next to the word.

...... sunny
...... hot
...... chilly
...... cloudy
...... rainy
...... windy
...... stormy
...... cold front

a
b
c
d

e
f
g
h

Before You Listen

Work with your partner. Look at the words. Write them on the line to show how certain the speaker is. Two are done for you.

■ might   ■ will probably   ■ is going to   ■ may   ■ is likely to   ■ will

Not Sure   Sure

| might | | | | | is going to |

Practice the dialogue. Talk about the coming week's weather. Choose your own words where the _____ is and talk about different days. You can use words from above.

A: Do you think it's going to be _____ on *Saturday?*

B: Yes, I do.

No. I think it _____ be _____ .

Let's Listen!

Listen to the weather forecast. Place a check (✓) to show what people living in the regions might want to do.

	Use sunglasses	Drink lots of water	Wear a coat	Take an umbrella
East Asia	☐	☐	☐	☐
The Pacific	☐	☐	☐	☐
The Middle East	☐	☐	☐	☐
North. Africa	☐	☐	☐	☐
Southern. Africa	☐	☐	☐	☐
Southern. Europe	☐	☐	☐	☐
Northern Europe	☐	☐	☐	☐

Check your answers with your partner.

꞉ Listen Again

Listen to the forecast again and write the letter(s) of the correct weather symbol (s) next to the region.

East Asia ....
The Pacific ....
The Middle East ......
Northern Africa ......
Southern Africa ....
Southern Europe ....
Northern Europe ....

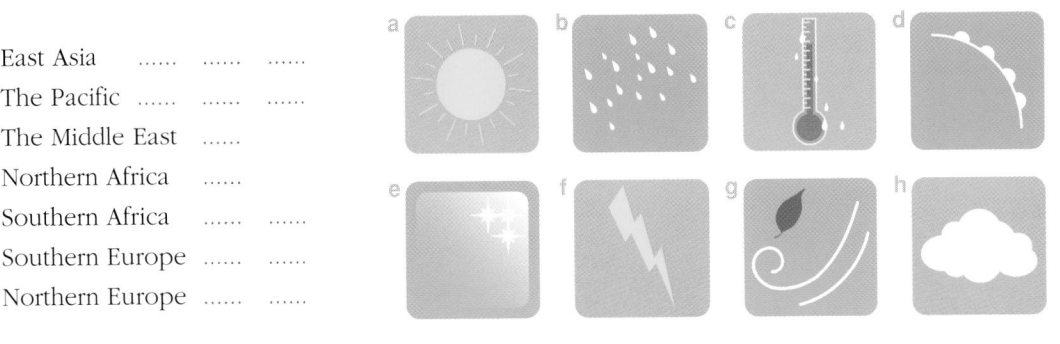

Check your answers with your partner.

꞉ Listening Clinic One: Stress and Certainty

Speakers can show how sure they are by where they put stress.

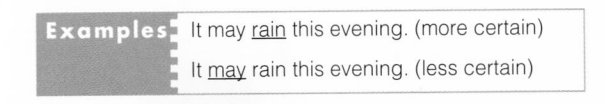

Examples It may <u>rain</u> this evening. (more certain)
It <u>may</u> rain this evening. (less certain)

Listen to the dialogue. Underline the words that are *stressed*.

A: You ready for the soccer game tomorrow?
B: But it's going to rain, isn't it?
A: No. But it might rain in the afternoon, so...
B: The weatherman said it will rain. And it'll snow as well.
A: I don't think you want to play, do you?
B: I could play but I may be seeing Jill tomorrow.

Check your answers with your partner. Now say the dialogue together.

꞉ Practice!

Work first on your own, then with your partner.

Student A: Look at the chart on the next page. Use your imagination and fill in the morning (a.m.) section of the chart. Write down the weather for each day of the week. You can use more than one word for each day and you can choose to be more certain or less certain.

Student B: Look at the chart on the next page. Use your imagination and fill in the afternoon (p.m.) section of the chart. Write down the weather for each day of the week. You can use more than one word for each day and you can choose to be more certain or less certain.

	Monday	Tuesday	Wednesday	Thursday	Friday
a.m.					
p.m.					

Now ask and answer questions with your partner. Ask what the weather will be like on each day. Write the weather s/he says. Answer your partner's questions. Change your stress to show how sure you are.

Now Listen Back

Look back at the map in *Let's Start!* Listen again and write down the high and low temperatures for each region.

Check your answers with your partner.

Listening Clinic Two: Stress and Certainty

Work with your partner. Listen to the sentences. Underline the stressed word(s) then decide together how sure the speaker is. Circle *More certain* or *Less certain*.

1. It's probably going to snow tonight.   More certain   Less certain

2. It's probably stopped raining.   More certain   Less certain

3. It's supposed to warm up later.   More certain   Less certain

4. It might get windy in the afternoon.   More certain   Less certain

5. Looks like we'll probably have a thunderstorm.   More certain   Less certain

6. It's likely to clear up later today.   More certain   Less certain

Now say the sentences.

Work in a group of three. Decide what the weather is usually like in your country in each season.

- ■ In spring it's usually ....
- ■ In summer it's usually ....
- ■ In fall it's usually ....
- ■ In winter it's usually ....

The following people are coming to your country for a holiday:

- ■ a married couple with a small child
- ■ a group on an adventure holiday
- ■ a group of high school students
- ■ a retired couple

Decide the following in your group:

- ■ When should they visit?
- ■ Where should they go?
- ■ What kind of clothes/other items will they probably need to bring?
- ■ How might the weather affect their holiday plans/choices?

Compare your ideas with a student from a different group.

Turn to page 109 and complete the word list. Use your dictionary if you want to.
Use the CD at the back of your book and listen to the recordings in this unit again. The script for this unit is on pages 93 and 94.

Unit 9 — Can I speak to Bill, please?

Let's Start!

Work in a group of three. Ask and answer the questions.

- How often do you use the phone?
- Who do you call most often?
- What time of day do you usually make calls?
- Do you have a cell phone?

Before You Listen

Work with your partner. Look at the expressions. Circle *C* if the person *calling* usually says it. Circle *R* if the person *receiving* the call usually says it.

Expression		
Could I speak to Bill please?	C	R
Is Bill there?	C	R
Just a minute, I'll get him.	C	R
I'm sorry, he's out.	C	R
When will he be back?	C	R
Can I have your name?	C	R
Could I leave a message?	C	R
Can I take a message?	C	R
Sorry, wrong number.	C	R
Could you tell him I called?	C	R

Compare your answers with another pair.

Let's Listen!

Listen to four telephone conversations. Draw lines and match the conversation with the reason for the call.

- get information

Conversation 1 ●
- ask if someone can do something

Conversation 2 ●
- change an appointment

Conversation 3 ●
- find out a meeting time

Conversation 4 ●
- invite someone
- make a reservation

Check your answers with your partner.

Listen to the conversations again. Circle the word to answer each question.

■ Do the speakers know each other?

Conversation 1	Yes	No
Conversation 2	Yes	No
Conversation 3	Yes	No
Conversation 4	Yes	No

■ Is the person called available?

Conversation 1	Yes	No
Conversation 2	Yes	No
Conversation 3	Yes	No
Conversation 4	Yes	No

■ Does the receiver take a message?

Conversation 1	Yes	No
Conversation 2	Yes	No
Conversation 3	Yes	No
Conversation 4	Yes	No

■ What is the relationship between the speakers?

Conversation 1	Personal	Business	Strangers
Conversation 2	Personal	Business	Strangers
Conversation 3	Personal	Business	Strangers
Conversation 4	Personal	Business	Strangers

⁞ Listening Clinic One: Lost Sounds and Lost Words

Sounds in and at the end of words are sometimes not spoken. Sometimes whole words are not spoken. They are lost.

> **Example** Have you seen Pete anywhere? → You seen Pete anywhere?
> (the word "have" is lost)

Listen to the dialogue. Draw lines through any words which are *lost*. Draw a slash (/) through any sounds which are *lost*.

A: Hello?

B: Jamie, this is Allen.

A: Allen. How are you doing?

B: Good. How about you?

A: Not bad. So, what's up?

B: Are you doing anything special this afternoon?

A: I don't know. Why?

Check your answers with your partner. Now say the dialogue together.

Work with your partner. Rewrite the dialogues so that they are more polite. The first part is done for you.

Telephone Call 1

A: Get Smith.   *Could I speak to Mr. Smith please?*

B: What?   ....

A: Get Smith.   ....

B: Who are you?   ....

A: Jones.   ....

B: Wait.   ....

A: Okay.   ....

      ....

Telephone Call 2

A: I'm Jones. Get Smith.   ....

B: What?   ....

A: I'm Jones. Get Smith.   ....

B: He's out.   ....

A: Take a message.   ....

B: Okay.   ....

A: Tell him to call back.   ....

B: Okay.   ....

A: Okay, bye.   ....

B: Bye.   ....

Now practice the dialogues together.

⁝Now Listen Back

Listen to the conversations again. Place a check (✓) next to the phrase that best describes the next step somebody has to take.

Conversation 1   ☐ meet each other   ☐ wait for someone to call back
                  ☐ give someone a message

Conversation 2   ☐ meet each other   ☐ wait for someone to call back
                  ☐ call someone back

Conversation 3   ☐ meet each other   ☐ wait for someone to call back
                  ☐ give someone a message

Conversation 4   ☐ meet each other   ☐ wait for someone to call back
                  ☐ give someone a message

Check your answers with your partner.

⚑ Listening Clinic Two: Lost Sounds and Lost Words

Work with your partner. Look at the sentences. Draw lines through any words and draw a slash (/) through any sounds that may be *lost*.

1. When are you going to be ready?
2. Where did he go yesterday?
3. Is John there?
4. Is it time to leave yet?
5. When did you get back?
6. What did he say?

Listen and check. Now say the sentences.

⚑ Try It Out!

Work with your partner. Follow the prompts on the next page and have a conversation. Take turns to be Student A and Student B.

Student A: You are Tim's mother/father. Tim is out. Answer the phone and take a message.

Student B: You missed school today because you were ill. Phone your friend, Tim. Ask him about homework.

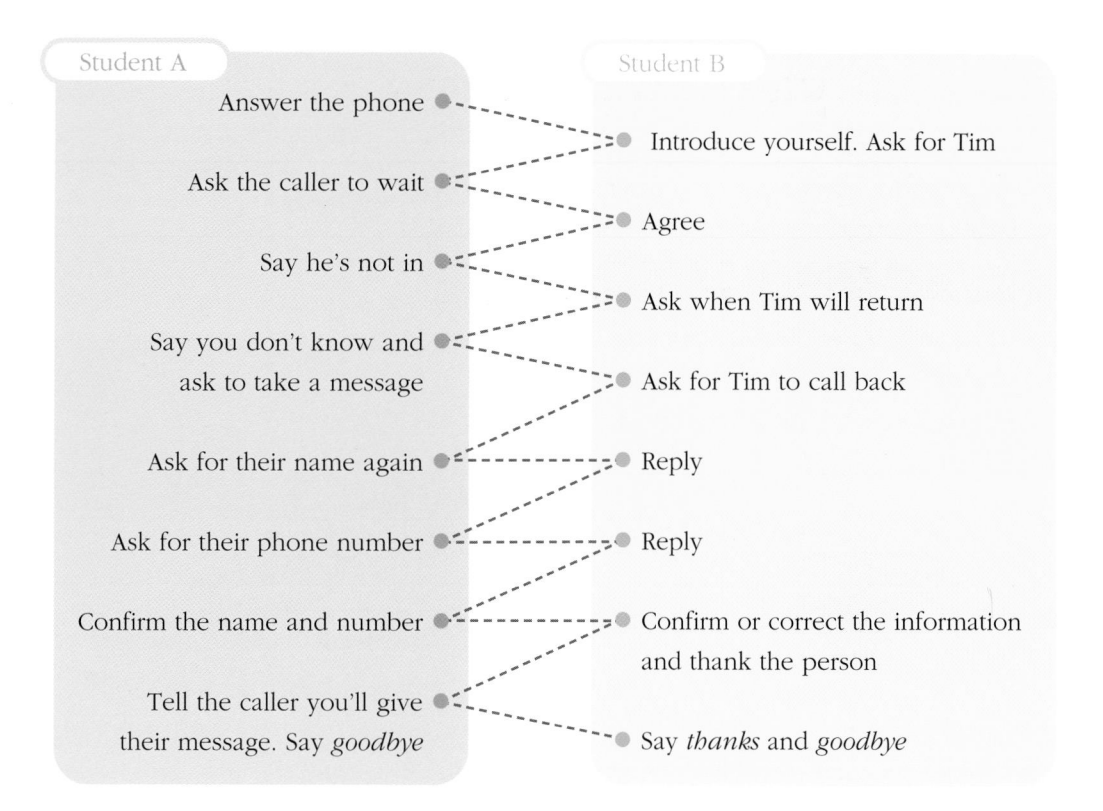

Student A

Answer the phone

Ask the caller to wait

Say he's not in

Say you don't know and
ask to take a message

Ask for their name again

Ask for their phone number

Confirm the name and number

Tell the caller you'll give
their message. Say *goodbye*

Student B

Introduce yourself. Ask for Tim

Agree

Ask when Tim will return

Ask for Tim to call back

Reply

Reply

Confirm or correct the information
and thank the person

Say *thanks* and *goodbye*

⊡ In Your Own Time

**Turn to pages 109 and 110 and complete the word list. Use your dictionary if you want to.
Use the CD at the back of your book and listen to the recordings in this unit again. The
script for this unit is on pages 94 and 95.**

Unit 10 — First day on the job

⊹ Let's Start!

Work on your own. Check (✓) your answers to the quiz.

- ■ Where did you first meet your best friend?
  - ☐ at school   ☐ at work
  - ☐ at a party   ☐ other

- ■ Which do you think is the best place to meet new people?
  - ☐ at school   ☐ at work
  - ☐ at a party   ☐ other

- ■ Do you enjoy meeting new people?
  - ☐ yes, a lot   ☐ sometimes   ☐ not really   ☐ no

- ■ How do you feel when you meet someone your age for the first time?
  - ☐ a bit shy   ☐ nervous   ☐ open   ☐ reserved   ☐ scared

- ■ How do you feel when you meet someone much older for the first time?
  - ☐ a bit shy   ☐ nervous   ☐ open   ☐ reserved   ☐ scared

- ■ What kinds of things do people talk about when they meet for the first time?
  - ☐ family   ☐ school or work
  - ☐ friends   ☐ where you are from
  - ☐ religion   ☐ politics
  - ☐ hobbies/interests   ☐ love

Work with your partner. Compare your answers to the quiz.

Work with your partner. Choose one phrase from each box and write your answers to complete the dialogues.

■ A: How are you doing?

  B: ....

  A: Can't complain.

- I'm pleased to meet you.
- Not bad. How about you?
- Very well, thanks. Yourself?
- How's it going?

■ A: ....

  B: I'm pleased to meet you, too.

- How are you doing?
- How's it going?
- It's very nice to meet you.
- It was a pleasure meeting you.

■ A: ....

  B: Great, thanks. You?

  A: ....

- It's a pleasure to meet you.
- What's up?   How's it going?
- How are you?

- Fine thank you. And you?
- Very well, thanks.   Not bad.
- Pretty good

■ A: ....

  B: Fine thank you. And yourself?

  A: ....

- How are you doing?
- I'm pleased to meet you.
- How's it going?   How do you do?

- Very well, thanks.
- Not bad.   Pretty good.
- It's a pleasure to meet you.

■ Which conversations are formal?
■ Which conversations are casual?

Now say the dialogues together.

Work with your partner. Check (✓) the reply which does not fit the introduction.

■ A: Paul, I'd like you to meet your supervisor, Andrea Garcia.
   B: ☐ I'm pleased to meet you.   ☐ Nice to meet you.   ☐ What's new?

■ A: Paul, this is Elaine Lincoln, our sales manager.
   B: ☐ It's a pleasure to meet you.   ☐ How's it going, Elaine?   ☐ Pleased to meet you.

■ A: Paul, have you met our sales manager?
   B: ☐ I don't think so. Hello, I'm...   ☐ Yes, we've already met.   ☐ What's up?

■ A: Paul, do you know Cynthia Morgan, our secretary?
   B: ☐ No, we haven't met.   ☐ Nice to meet you.   ☐ It's a great honor to meet you, Ms. Morgan.

⁝ **Let's Listen!**

Listen to three conversations. Paul Smothers is starting his first day at *Great Lakes Magazine.* He is meeting some of the staff. Draw lines from the person on the left to his/her job title.

Title
- Secretary
- Assistant Manager
- Features Editor
- Delivery Manager
- Editor
- Summer Assistant
- Sales Manager

Name
Andrea Garcia ●
Elaine Lincoln ●
Cindi Morgan ●
Paul Smothers ●

Check your answers with your partner.

⁝ **Listen Again**

Listen to the three conversations again. Place a check (✓) next to the phrases you hear the people use to introduce and greet one another.

Converation 1
☐ *Let me introduce you to...*   ☐ *I don't think so.*
☐ *Thank you very much.*   ☐ *Nice to meet you.*
☐ *I'd like you to meet...*   ☐ *I'm pleased to meet you.*
☐ *This is...*   ☐ *You, too.*

☐ *This is…*　　　　☐ *We've already met.*

☐ *Hi.*　　　　☐ *I'm pleased to meet you.*

☐ *I'd like you to meet…*　　　　☐ *How do you do?*

☐ *Have you met…?*　　　　☐ *Nice to meet you.*

Conversation 3

☐ *This is…*　　　　☐ *You, too.*

☐ *Let me introduce you to…*　　　　☐ *Nice to meet you.*

☐ *Have you met…?*　　　　☐ *I'm pleased to meet you.*

☐ *Do you know…?*　　　　☐ *I don't think so.*

Check your answers with your partner.

⏵Listening Clinic One: Changing Sounds

Sounds in words sometimes change in natural speech. This is especially common with the /t/ sound.

Example	I'd like you to mee**t** our president → I'd like you to mee**d** our president
	(the /t/ in *meet* changes to a /d/)

Listen to the dialogue. Circle the places where sounds *change*.

A: Kathi. Hi. Have you got a minute?

B: Can you wait a second?

A: Sure. Take your time.

B: I've just got to put away my files. Okay. Sorry about that.

A: I want you to meet our new staff member, Paul.

B: Good to meet you. I'm Kathi.

Check your answers with your partner. Now say the dialogue together.

⏵Practice!

Work in a group of three and practice introducing each other. Take turns to be Student A.

Student A: Choose either a formal or informal greeting and introduce Student B to Student C.

Students B and C: Greet one another.

Listen to the three conversations again. Draw lines and match the people to their connection with Paul then answer the two questions.

Andrea Garcia ●

Elaine Lincoln ●

Cindi Morgan ●

● is from Paul's hometown

● went to the same college as Paul

● has a brother who knows Paul

● went to college in Paul's hometown

● is a family friend

Who sounds the most friendly?   ....

Who sounds the most formal?   ....

Compare your answers with your partner.

Listening Clinic Two: Changing Sounds

Work with your partner. Look at the sentences. Circle the places where a /t/ may *change* to a /d/.

1. What is he going to say at the meeting?
2. I've got to turn off my computer.
3. She went downstairs to get a package they sent us.
4. I'm sorry, but I've got a meeting right now.
5. We've got a lot to do today.
6. Let's start out with the easy stuff first.

Listen and check. Now say the sentences.

⁑Try It Out!

Work in a group of three. Look at the situations. Decide if the situation is formal or casual, then decide what each person should say. Choose a role, and practice meeting and greeting.

Situation 1

You're meeting a group of your friend's friends at a party.
Roles: Friend/Friend's friend/ You

Situation 2

You're meeting an old friend of your father's for the first time at an expensive restaurant.
Roles: Father/You/ Father's Friend

Situation 3

Your friend is introducing you to a girl/boy.
You're at a coffee shop.
Roles: You/Your friend/A mystery date

Choose one of the situations and prepare a short sketch.
Act out your sketch to another group.

⁑In Your Own Time

Turn to page 110 and complete the word list. Use your dictionary if you want to.
Use the CD at the back of your book and listen to the recordings in this unit again.
The script for this unit is on pages 95 and 96.

I'm interested in taking a course

Let's Start!

Work in a group of three. Look at the advertisements and discuss the questions.

KARATE learn the Japanese art of self-defense in just six months.	**ENGLISH CLASSES** all levels, intensive courses, business English, much more.	**BASIC COMPUTING** four-week introduction to email and key software.

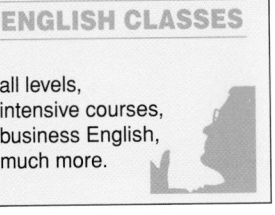

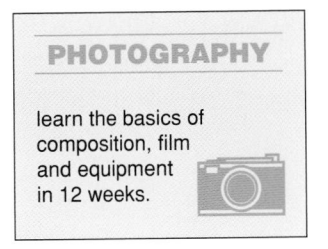

PHOTOGRAPHY learn the basics of composition, film and equipment in 12 weeks.

TENNIS learn the basics of the game in a small group in only two months.

Which courses are you interested in? Why?

What do you think you might need to bring from home for each of these courses?

Words

Work with your partner. Draw lines and match the definitions on the left with the words on the right.

money you pay to go to school ●   ● enrol

course for middle-level students ●   ● advanced

money for rent and food ●   ● student visa

to enter a school ●   ● tuition

course for high-level students ●   ● room and board

a form or stamp a country gives ●   ● intermediate
that lets you study there

Check your answers with another pair.

Work in a group of three. Make a list of some things you need to know about a course before enrolling. Two are done for you.

cost of the course
the day the course is on
....
....
....
....

Compare your ideas with a student from another group.

Let's Listen!

Listen to the conversation. Place a check (✓) next to the questions that the student asks about the English course.

☐ *What are the dates for the course?*
☐ *Is there a lot of homework?*
☐ *How much do the textbooks cost?*
☐ *How many students are there per class?*
☐ *Do I have to have a student visa?*
☐ *How much does the course cost?*
☐ *What do I need to bring to class?*
☐ *What is the level of the course?*
☐ *Could you send me an application form?*

Check your answers with your partner.

Listen Again

Listen to the conversation again. Complete the table with information about the course.

Course title: ....
Dates: ....
Days: ....
Times: ....
Cost: ....
Class size: ....
Facilities: ....

Check your answers with your partner.

⯈Listening Clinic One: Intonation in Questions

Closed questions are when the number of possible replies is limited. They usually have a falling intonation.

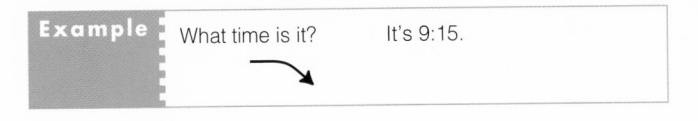

Open questions are when the number of possible responses is large. They usually have a rising intonation.

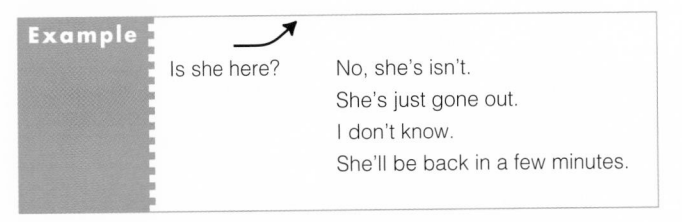

Listen to the dialogue. Draw (⬊) if the speaker's intonation *falls* on the questions. Draw (⬈) if the speaker's intonation *rises* on the questions.

A: May I help you?

B: Yes, I think I'd like to take a course.

A: Which one?

B: General English. When does the course begin?

A: The next one starts in three weeks.

B: Do I need a student visa?

Check your answers with your partner. Now say the dialogue together.

⯈Practice!

Work with your partner. Look back at the advertisements in *Let's Start!* Take turns to ask questions about the courses. Use your imagination and answer your partner's questions.

Listen to the conversation again. Check (✓) the words or phrases to show your opinion of Hudson College.

Type of course:	☐ boring		☐ interesting		☐ useful
Course length:	☐ too short		☐ too long		☐ about right
Cost:	☐ fair		☐ a bit expensive		☐ too much
Class time:	☐ too early in the day		☐ too late in the day		☐ fine
Facilities:	☐ not enough		☐ average		☐ quite good

Compare your answers with your partner.

Would you like to study English at Hudson College? Why (not)?

⊦Listening Clinic Two: Intonation in Questions

Work with your partner. Look at the sentences. Draw (↘) if the speaker's intonation may *fall* on the questions. Draw (↗) if the speaker's intonation may *rise* on the questions.

1. May I help you?
2. Do I need a visa?
3. Does it take long?
4. So it could be longer?
5. Is that five days a week?
6. What time does the class start?

Listen and check. Now say the questions.

Try It Out!

Work with your partner. Student A: Turn to page 97. Student B: Turn to page 99.

In Your Own Time

Turn to pages 110 and and 111 and complete the word list. Use your dictionary if you want to. Use the CD at the back of your book and listen to the recordings in this unit again. The script for this unit is on pages 96, 97 and 98.

Unit 12 — What time do we arrive?

Let's Start!

Work with your partner. Look at the pictures and answer the questions.

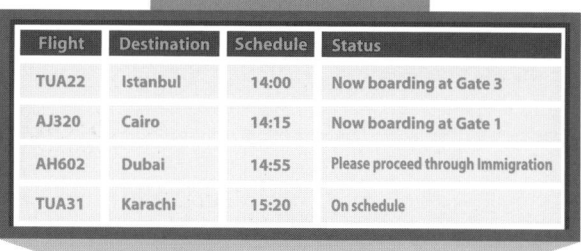

Flight	Destination	Schedule	Status
TUA22	Istanbul	14:00	Now boarding at Gate 3
AJ320	Cairo	14:15	Now boarding at Gate 1
AH602	Dubai	14:55	Please proceed through Immigration
TUA31	Karachi	15:20	On schedule

ARRIVALS

TRANSIT PASSENGERS ONLY

What are these pictures of?

What place(s) do you see them?

Is there any information on arriving flights?

How many flights are shown leaving? Where are they flying to?

Compare your answers with another pair.

Before You Listen

Work in a group of three. You want to go to Thailand. You are going to call a travel agent. Make a list of the information you need. Make a list of the things the travel agent will probably ask you about. One is done for you.

You need to know:

- ☐ ....
- ☐ ....
- ☐ ....
- ☐ ....
- ☐ ....
- ☐ ....

The travel agent needs to know:

- ☐ *your name*
- ☐ ....
- ☐ ....
- ☐ ....
- ☐ ....
- ☐ ....

Compare your ideas with a student from another group.

Let's Listen!

Listen to a conversation between a customer and a travel agent. Place a check (✓) next to the items in your list from *Before You Listen* that the speakers mention.

Check your answers with your partner.

⯀ Listen Again

Listen to Part 3 of the conversation again. Complete the table.

	Flight out	Return flight 1	Return flight 2 (first leg)	(second leg)
Flight number:			UA 763	UA 763
Departs (city):				
Departure date:	August 3			
Departure time:		5:30 a.m.		5:30 p.m.
Arrives (city):	San Francisco		Tokyo	
Arrival date:				
Arrival time:				

Check your answers with your partner.

⯀ Listening Clinic One: Lost Sounds and Strong or Weak?

Speakers put stress on words which are important. Sometimes speakers don't pronounce all the sounds in the words.

> **Example**
> What do we need to do at the airport?
> → Whu du we need tu do ut the airport?

Listen to the dialogue. Circle the words that are *stressed*. Draw a slash (/) through sounds that are *lost*.

A: ... and your first name was?
B: Aaron.
A: ... and what's your nationality?
B: Canadian.
A: ... and your date of birth?
B: It's the 26th of June, 1964.
A: Okay, let's see what we can do for you.

Check your answers with your partner. Now say the dialogue together.

⁝Practice!

Work with your partner. Student A: Turn to page 101. Student B: Turn to page 104.

⁝Now Listen Back

Listen to the conversation again. Circle the word(s) that best completes the sentence.

■ The travel agent mistakes the customer's...	first name.	last name.
■ The flight the customer wanted is...	full.	cancelled.
■ The travel agent mistakes the...	price of the tickets.	number of tickets.
■ There are no .... available on the 24th.	flights	seats
■ The customer has to return...	later than she wants to.	earlier than she wants to.

Which of the two return flights do you think Mrs. Bixby will choose? Why?
Which flight would you choose?

Check and compare your answers with your partner.

⁝Listening Clinic Two: Lost Sounds and Strong Or Weak?

Work with your partner. Look at the sentences. Underline the vowels which may become *weak*. Draw a slash (/) through sounds which may be *lost*.

1. When you get to the airport, go to the counter.
2. Show your tickets and passports to the agent.
3. Check your bags, and get your boarding cards.
4. Don't put the passports in your suitcase.
5. And don't lose your baggage claim tickets.
6. When you arrive, they'll give you a tourist visa.

Listen and check. Now say the sentences.

▶Try It Out!

Work with your partner. Roleplay booking a flight. Take Turns to be the customer and the travel agent.

Customer: You are planning a trip to Spain. There are flights from your city to the cities of Madrid and Barcelona in Spain. You want to leave on October 16, 17 or 18. Before you begin, choose which city and which date you prefer. You can use the following expressions:

I want to book a flight to ▭ *.*

Do you have anything cheaper?

Do you have anything leaving earlier/later?

How about…

Travel Agent: Look at the information in the timetable to answer the customer's questions. Before you begin, cross out three flights. You cannot sell tickets for these flights as they are full. You can use the following expressions:

May I help you?

One moment please.

We have a flight leaving at ▭ *on the* ▭ *.*

I'm sorry, there are no flights to ▭ *available on the* ▭ *.*

I'm sorry, that's all we have.

Destination: Madrid

Date	Flight No.	Departure	Arrival	Cost
Oct. 16	TUA11	7:15 a.m.	12:35 p.m.	$649
Oct. 16	AH141	5:20 p.m.	10:45 p.m.	$675
Oct. 17	TUA11	7:15 a.m.	12:35 p.m.	$649
Oct. 17	AJ716	9:50 a.m.	1:20 a.m.*	$539
Oct. 18	TUA11	7:15 a.m.	12:35 p.m.	$649
Oct. 18	TUA12	2:25 p.m.	7:45 p.m.	$649

Destination: Barcelona

Date	Flight No.	Departure	Arrival	Cost
Oct. 16	AH131	11:20 a.m.	5:15 p.m.	$660
Oct. 16	TUA17	7:45 a.m.	1:05 p.m.	$649
Oct. 18	AJ773	6:20 a.m.	12:15 p.m.	$589
Oct. 18	TUA17	7:45 a.m.	1:05 p.m.	$649

*Oct. 18 (change planes in Casablanca)

▶In Your Own Time

Turn to page 111 and complete the word list. Use your dictionary if you want to.
Use the CD at the back of your book and listen to the recordings in this unit again. The script for this unit is on pages 98, 99 and 100.

Rules of the house

⊹ Let's Start!

Work on your own. Imagine that a friend of yours comes to stay at your house. How would you feel if s/he did the following things? Circle your answers. *1* (don't mind so much) to *4* (quite annoyed).

■ uses your toothbrush	1	2	3	4
■ invites people over without asking	1	2	3	4
■ takes very long baths	1	2	3	4
■ does not offer to help with chores	1	2	3	4
■ smokes in your bedroom	1	2	3	4
■ doesn't make the bed	1	2	3	4
■ makes a long-distance phone call	1	2	3	4
■ bullies your dog	1	2	3	4
■ comes home well after midnight	1	2	3	4

Compare your answers with your partner.

Which of the actions is the most/least serious? Why do you think so?

⊹ Words

Work with your partner. Complete the sentences with a suitable word or phrase.

- ■ show (someone) around
- ■ keep the volume down
- ■ turn off
- ■ time difference
- ■ wash

- ■ invite (someone) over
- ■ lock
- ■ knock
- ■ fridge
- ■ put away

- ■ Can you ...., Paul? I'm trying to do my homework.
- ■ The kettle's boiling. .... the gas please, Peter.
- ■ The .... between Japan and Korea is one hour.
- ■ If you ...., I'll dry the dishes.
- ■ What a mess! Can you .... your CDs, clothes and stuff, please?
- ■ Make sure you put the milk back in the .... after you use it.
- ■ Don't walk straight into the bedroom. Always .... first.
- ■ Please .... the windows before you go to bed.
- ■ Let's .... Jim and Suzy .... for brunch this Sunday.
- ■ Terry, can you .... Judith ....? It's her first day here.

Match each picture below to the correct sentence.

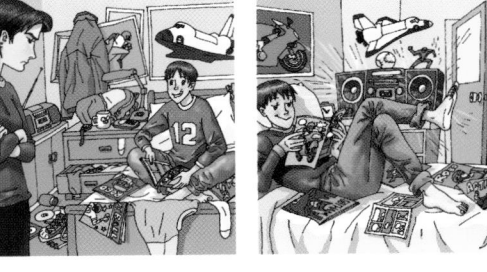

⋮ Let's Listen!

Listen to the conversation. Check (✓) the phrase to complete each sentence.

- ■ The speakers are…   ☐ homeowner and inspector.   ☐ guest and homeowner.
- ■ They…   ☐ have just met.   ☐ have met before.
- ■ The woman is…   ☐ explaining rules.   ☐ making up new rules.
- ■ They talk about rules for…   ☐ two rooms.   ☐ three rooms.   ☐ four rooms.

Check your answers with your partner.

⋮ Listen Again

Listen to the conversation again. Look at the pictures. Circle the activities which are breaking the house rules.

Check your answers with your partner.

⯈ Listening Clinic One: Intonation: Finished or Not Finished?

When the speaker's voice falls, it usually means s/he has finished speaking. When the speaker's voice is going up, it usually means s/he has not finished speaking.

Examples	
	I'm sorry...　I didn't...　Could I possibly...　Excuse me... (not finished)
	I'm sorry...　That's okay...　Excuse me... (finished)

Listen to the dialogue. Circle *F* if the speaker has *finished speaking*. Circle *UF* if the speaker has *not finished speaking*.

A: Sure. Is there anything else?	F	UF
B: Well, there is one more thing.	F	UF
A: What?	F	UF
B: Would it be okay to have some friends over?	F	UF
A: Today? I'd rather you didn't, not today, anyway.	F	UF
B: Okay, I see.	F	UF

Check your answers with your partner. Now say the dialogue together.

⯈ Practice!

Work on your own. Imagine a student is coming to stay at your house. Look at the list. Which of the things will you allow the guest to do? Which are not okay? Check (✓) *Yes* or *No*.

	Yes	No
▪ smoke in the living room	☐	☐
▪ smoke in their own room	☐	☐
▪ turn up the heat	☐	☐
▪ eat snacks in their room	☐	☐
▪ have a party	☐	☐
▪ play music loudly	☐	☐
▪ watch TV late at night	☐	☐
▪ use the washing machine	☐	☐
▪ invite friends over	☐	☐
▪ bring a pet	☐	☐

Work with your partner. Compare your ideas by asking questions. Use the question prompts to help you.

Is it okay to...?　　　*Do you mind if guests...?*　　　*Can guests...?*

∴ Now Listen Back

Listen to the conversation again. Write down which rules you think are:

fair ....

a bit strict ....

too strict ....

for safety ....

silly ....

Compare your answers with your partner.

Would you like to stay with Mrs. Weiss? Why (not)?

∴ Listening Clinic Two: Intonation: Finished or Not Finished?

Work with your partner. Look at the dialogue. Write *F* where you think the speaker may have *finished speaking*. Write *UF* where you think the speaker has *not finished speaking*.

.... A: If everyone's ready... First, does anyone have any questions? Okay then

.... B: Excuse me

.... A: I'm sorry. Do you have a question

.... B: I want to know

.... A: I'm sorry, you want to know

.... B: I want to know if we have to be here at 9:00 tomorrow

Listen and check. Now say the dialogue together.

Work in two groups. Group A: You are looking for a suitable host family. Group B: You are homeowners offering homestays.

Group A: Decide what kind of host family you want to stay with.

Group B: Think of the rules you want to have in your home.

Use these ideas if you like. Use your own ideas as well.

- smoking
- staying out late
- inviting friends over
- playing music loudly
- making long phone calls
- coming and going without telling anyone
- taking long showers
- watching a lot of TV

Now work with students from the other group.

Group A: Try to find the house that is most suitable for you.

Group B: Try to find the best guest for your house.

Now go back to your group and discuss the questions with a partner.

Could I have my own key.

Can my friends stay over sometimes?

Sure you can.

I'm afraid that's not possible.

Can I bring my cat?

I'm sorry but no pets.

Group A
Did you find a suitable house?
What silly rules did you hear?

Group B
Did you find a suitable guest?
What silly requests did you hear?

Turn to pages 111 and 112 and complete the word list. Use your dictionary if you want to. Use the CD at the back of your book and listen to the recordings in this unit again. The script for this unit is on pages 100 and 101.

Unit 14 Haven't you changed

⊦Let's Start!

Work with your partner. Ask and answer the questions.

- Do you look more like your mother, father or another relative?
- How is your appearance different compared to five years ago?
- What do you look like now? Can you describe yourself?

⊦Words

Work with your partner. Match the words to the pictures of the people.

- overweight
- thin
- skinny
- tan
- pale
- perm
- thick hair

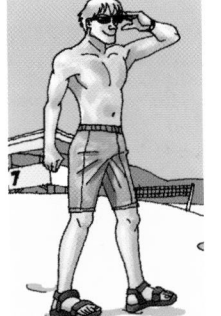

Circle the phrase shown by the two pictures below.

- lose weight
- gain weight

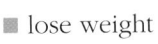

Work on your own. Place a check (✓) next to statements that are true about you.

☐ I want to change my hairstyle.
☐ I want to dye my hair.
☐ I'm heavier than I was a year ago.
☐ I'm taller than I was a year ago.
☐ I want to lose weight.
☐ I want to get contact lenses.
☐ My appearance is very important to me.

Work in a group of three. Compare your answers. Ask questions.

Let's Listen!

Listen to the conversation. Amelia and Suzanne are old friends. They are talking about how their appearance has changed. Choose from the pictures. Place a cross (✗) next to the picture that shows what each woman used to look like (*Before*). Place a check (✓) next to the picture that shows how each woman looks *Now*.

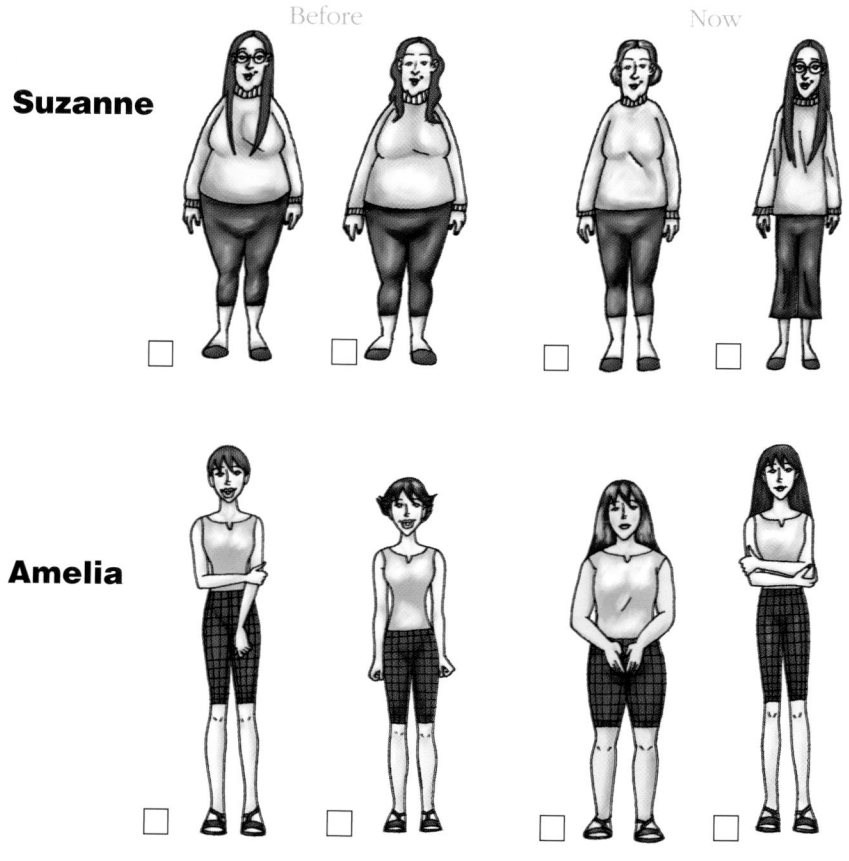

⦂ Listen Again

Listen to the conversation again. Circle the words to show what Amelia and Suzanne looked like in high school (*Then*) and today (*Now*).

Suzanne:	Then			Now		
Size:	skinny	thin	overweight	lost weight	gained weight	same weight
Hair:	long	short	really short	long	short	really short
Eyes:	glasses	contacts		glasses	contacts	
Hair color:	brown	colored		brown	colored	

Amelia:	Then			Now		
Size:	skinny	thin	overweight	lost weight	gained weight	same weight
Hair:	long	short	really short	long	short	really short
Makeup:	more	less	the same	more	less	the same
Skin tone:	pale	tan		pale	tan	

Check your answers with your partner.

⦂ Listening Clinic One: Shared Sounds

When a word ends with the a sound and the next word starts with the same sound, the two words usually share the sound.

Example	I found a magazine with these pictures of famous celebrities
	→ I found a magazine wi-th-ese pictures of famou-s-elebrities

Listen to the dialogue. Circle places where two words *share a sound*.

A: I really eat too much. I've got to go on a diet.

B: You ought to get some more exercise, too.

A: Exercise? I've got too much to do already.

B: You ought to swim, maybe even try jogging?

A: I ought to get some rest!

B: If you don't at least try to exercise, you won't take off any weight.

Check your answers with your partner. Now say the dialogue together.

Work with your partner. Look at the pictures. Describe some of the people. Try to guess who your partner is describing. Take turns to describe and to guess.

⊹Now Listen Back

Listen to the conversation again and circle your answer to the question.

Who is happier with her appearance now?   Amelia   Suzanne

Compare your answer with your partner.

⊹Listening Clinic Two: Shared Sounds

Work with your partner. Look at the sentences. Circle places where two words may *share a sound.*

1. He's so thin, now.
2. She's still not too tall for her age.
3. He's still quite good-looking.
4. She's short, with thick, curly red hair.
5. I've got to go on a another diet. I'll start tomorrow.
6. There really isn't much chance he'll lose weight.

Listen and check. Now say the sentences.

⏷ Try It Out!

Work as a class. Ask four other students what they looked like five years ago compared to today. Use these questions to help you and write the answers in the table.

- Were you shorter (five years ago)?
- Did you wear more make-up (five years ago)?
- What kind of hairstyle did you use to have?
- What kind of clothes did you use to like wearing?

	Height	Weight	Hair Style	Biggest Change
Student 1	....	....	....	....
Student 2	....	....	....	....
Student 3	....	....	....	....
Student 4	....	....	....	....

Work in a group of three. Compare your information.

Which student has changed the most?

⏷ In Your Own Time

Turn to page 112 and complete the word list. Use your dictionary if you want to. Use the CD at the back of your book and listen to the recordings in this unit again. The script for this unit is on page 102.

Unit 15 Going away for the summer?

Let's Start!

Work on your own. Look at the different ways you can spend a vacation. Rank them in order from *1* (not my taste at all) to *6* (I really like this). Then place a check (✓) to answer the question.

- ▪ a few days at a beach resort   ....
- ▪ walking in the mountains   ....
- ▪ traveling abroad   ....
- ▪ studying something   ....
- ▪ adventure holidays   ....
- ▪ lazing around the house   ....

- ▪ Who do you like to take a vacation with?

  ☐ nobody, just myself   ☐ a group of friends   ☐ a girl/boyfriend   ☐ the family

Compare your answers with your partner. Do you have similar ideas?

Words and Expressions

Work with your partner. Draw lines from the beginning on the left to the end on the right and make eight sentences. The first one is done for you.

If you find a quiet place to have a holiday you can... ●	● stay home.
The beach is a great place to... ●	● try to get some exercise.
A lot of students... ●	● get away from it all.
I don't want to go out tonight, I want to... ●	● hang out with their friends after school.
Teenagers usually like to... ●	● going for a hike in the mountains.
If you're overweight you should... ●	● you'll get a tan.
If you lie in the sun for a few hours... ●	● relax and take it easy.
There's no better exercise than... ●	● work part-time to make some pocket money.

Check your answers with another pair.

Before You Listen

Work with your partner. Put these words and expressions in the correct place on the line. The first two are done for you.

- might
- may (well)
- will probably
- is likely to
- is going to
- doubt if

Not Sure   **Sure**

doubt if   *is going to*

Check your answers with your teacher.

Let's Listen!

Listen to two conversations. Look at the pictures. Who wants to do what? Who has to do what? Write the number of the picture(s) next to the person.

Conversation 1

Judy   ....

Eric   ....

Conversation 2

Ian   ....

Chrissy   ....

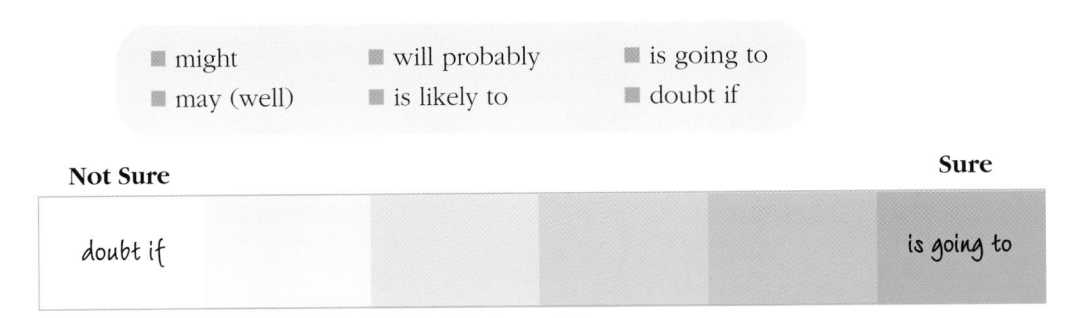

Check your answers with your partner.

:Listen Again

Listen to the conversations again. Circle the letter to show show certain each speaker is about their vacation plans. (*J* = Judy, *E* = Eric, *I* = Ian, *C* = Chrissy)

Conversation 1	Not certain	Quite certain	Certain
■ travel	J E	J E	J E
■ get away from it all	J E	J E	J E
■ relax and take it easy	J E	J E	J E
■ stay home	J E	J E	J E
■ surf the Net	J E	J E	J E
■ go to the beach	J E	J E	J E
■ work	J E	J E	J E

Conversation 2	Not certain	Quite certain	Certain
■ travel	I C	I C	I C
■ stay home	I C	I C	I C
■ go to the beach	I C	I C	I C
■ work	I C	I C	I C
■ go to the mountains	I C	I C	I C
■ read	I C	I C	I C
■ hike	I C	I C	I C
■ watch TV	I C	I C	I C

Check your answers with your partner.

:Listening Clinic One: A Final Look (1)

Work with your partner. Look at the dialogue. Circle places where you may find examples of the following points which you have studied in the *Listening Clinic* sections in this book.

Lost Sounds	Helping Sounds	Weak Vowels
Mixed Sounds	Shared Sounds	Joined Sounds

A: Do you have to take any more exams?

B: Yeah, I have got to take one more.

A: What are you going to do this summer?

B: I'm probably going to get a part-time job.

A: Is that what do you want to do?

B: Nah, but I really have to make some money.

Check your answers with your partner. Now say the dialogue together.

⊹ Practice!

Work with your partner. Talk about your plans for the weekend. Practice the dialogue. Choose your own words where the ▓▓▓▓ is.

A: Hi, ▓▓▓▓ . So what are you doing on the weekend? Any plans?

B: I'm not sure. I wanted to ▓▓▓▓ but I doubt if I'll be able to. I'll probably ▓▓▓▓ .

A: That sounds ▓▓▓▓ .

B: How about you, ▓▓▓▓ ? Are you going to ▓▓▓▓ ?

A: I don't know. I might. But I may also ▓▓▓▓ .

⊹ Now Listen Back

Listen to the conversations again. Place a check (✓) next to the speaker's name to answer the three questions.

■ Who is most excited about his/her vacation?

☐ Judy   ☐ Eric   ☐ Ian   ☐ Chrissy

■ Who is not excited about his/her vacation?

☐ Judy   ☐ Eric   ☐ Ian   ☐ Chrissy

■ Whose vacation plans are still not decided?

☐ Judy   ☐ Eric   ☐ Ian   ☐ Chrissy

Check your answers with your partner.

⊹ Listening Clinic Two: A Final Look (2)

Listen to the sentences. Circle the number of words in each sentence. Contractions (for example *she's*) count as two words.

1.	5	6	7
2.	6	7	8
3.	6	7	8
4.	7	8	9
5.	5	6	7
6.	5	6	7

Check your answers with your partner.

Turn to page 103 and say the sentences.

⋟Try It Out!

Work in a group of three. Look at the situation and decide about Mr. and Mrs. Kelley's holiday.

Mr. and Mrs. Kelley, a well-off, retired British couple in their early sixties are coming to your country for a three-week holiday. Think about places they might like to visit and the things they might like to do. Complete the table with your ideas.

Mr. Kelley:

■ Interested in history and old places
■ Likes to take long walks
■ Doesn't like places that are too hot

Mrs. Kelley:

■ Interested in culture
■ Likes to draw landscapes
■ Likes to try new things and meet new people

	Doubt	Might	Will probably	Going to
■ cities to visit	....	....	....	....
■ famous attractions	....	....	....	....
■ food	....	....	....	....
■ arts and culture	....	....	....	....
■ shopping	....	....	....	....
■ hotels	....	....	....	....
■ sports and activities	....	....	....	....

Compare your ideas with a student from a different group. How many of your ideas are the same?

⋟In Your Own Time

Turn to pages 112 and 113 and complete the word list. Use your dictionary if you want to. Use the CD at the back of your book and listen to the recordings in this unit again. The script for this unit is on pages 102 and 103.

Scripts

Unit 1: It's famous for soccer

Description 1

Okay, this country is an island. It's in Asia, It's famous for making cars, computers, cameras, stereos and TVs. It's a bit bigger than Italy. Most of the people live in cities. The capital is Tokyo and a famous place you may know is Mount Fuji.

Description 2

Now, this is the biggest country in South America. When you think of this country, you think of samba music, coffee and beautiful beaches. The people are also very good at soccer. There's a big festival in February or March called *Carnival*, with loud music, costumes, dancing and parades.

Description 3

Right, this one's in North Africa and it's quite large. It's very, very old, and famous for its history and culture. The capital is Cairo and the longest river in the world goes through this country. Some famous places tourists visit are the Sphinx and the Great Pyramids.

Description 4

So, here's the next country. It's in Europe, and it's well-known for the food, the wine, and, of course, the fashion. It's also famous for its culture and language, which is spoken in many countries around the world. The people are famous for being stylish and romantic, but a bit cool to outsiders. One famous place I'm sure you know is the Eiffel Tower.

Description 5

Okay, here's the fifth country. This one's the second-largest country in Asia, and it's famous for its history, culture and food. Hundreds of different languages are spoken here. More movies are made here than in any other country in a city people call *Bollywood*. The north of the country has some of the highest mountains in the world. A place you probably know is the Taj Mahal.

Description 6

Here's the last one. This country's in Europe but it's an island. A lot of foreign students come here to study, especially from Europe and Asia. It's famous for its writers, the royal family, pop music, and the countryside. Buckingham Palace and Big Ben are two popular tourist attractions.

Unit 2: How have you been?

Todd: Hey Glen. What's up?

Glen: Ah, not much, um, just finished classes. Oh, er... do you know Eric?

Todd: Yeah, we've been in some classes together. How's it going?

Eric: Pretty good I guess. Ah, how about you?

Todd: Not bad I guess.

Glen: So, er... what's new with you, Todd?

Todd: Ah, you know, same as usual. Listen, what are you guys doing tonight, cos there's this...

Glen: I've got to go to the library.

Todd: Homework?

Glen: Nah, we've got a test tomorrow so....

Todd: Oh, I was hoping we could go out later on tonight. You busy tonight, Eric?

Eric: Yeah, I've got to take the same test.

Glen: Okay, well. See you later.

Conversation 2

Elaine: Excuse me? John? John Stevens?

John: Elaine!

Elaine: I thought it was you. How have you been?

John: Very well, thank you. How about yourself?

Elaine: Fine, thank you. It's been a while, hasn't it?

John: It sure has. How are Simon and the children?

Elaine: They're all fine. How's Kate these days?

John: She's okay and the boys are, too.

Elaine: I'm glad to hear that. How's business?

John: Pretty good. I'm busy all the time though.

Elaine: Me too. Actually I've got an appointment upstairs and I'm late. Look, here's my card.
          Perhaps you could ask Kate to call me. Let's try to get together.

John: I'll do that. Hey listen, why don't you come over this weekend? We're having a barbecue.

Elaine: Sounds great. Call me, yeah? Got to go. Bye.

John: Bye. Good seeing you.

Conversation 3

Risa: Hi Mary, how are you doing? Sorry. I'm late.

Mary: Ah, that's okay.

Risa: Have you been here long?

Mary: I just got here. I haven't ordered yet. Are you hungry?

Risa: Yeah, a little. I'd love a drink first though.

Mary: Me too. Waiter? Two martinis and could you bring another menu?

Waiter: Of course madam.

Risa: So, what's new? How's work?

Mary:	Oh, pretty good. Guess what?
Risa:	What? Go on. Tell me.
Mary:	I got promoted.
Risa:	Hey, that's great news. When?
Mary:	Just heard on Monday.
Risa:	Congratulations.
Mary:	Thanks. I'm really pleased. How about you? How's work?
Risa:	A bit slow. I can't complain, though.
Terry:	Well, good evening ladies. Long time, no see.
Risa:	Hi!
Mary:	Hi, Terry. How have you been?
Terry:	Oh, not bad. This is a friend of mine, Art. Art, Risa and Mary.
Art:	How are you doing tonight?
M/R:	Fine/Not bad.
Art:	So, Terry tells me you guys used to work together at...

Conversation 4

Mr. Philips:	Beth? H-h... How are you? How have you been?
Beth:	Mr. Philips... Fine, thanks... and yourself?
Mr. Philips:	Oh, fine, thanks. It's been a while, hasn't it?
Beth:	Yes, it has...
Mr. Philips:	Er... would you care for something to drink?
Beth:	Oh, no thank you. I'm waiting for a... for a friend.
Mr. Philips:	Er... so, what have you been doing? How's the new job?
Beth:	Very interesting. We're quite busy at the moment.
Mr. Philips:	Well, erm... it's wonderful to see you again Beth, really.
Beth:	You too Mr. Philips. All the best, then.
Mr. Philips:	Yes well, I won't keep you.
Beth:	Nice to see you again. Goodbye.
Mr. Philips:	Goodbye then.

Unit 3: Can I help you ma'am?

Conversation 1

Sales Clerk:	Good morning sir. How are we doing today?
Customer:	Er... we're pretty good thanks.
Sales Clerk:	You're interested in the car navigators?
Customer:	Mmm. Not really, I'm jus... just looking thanks.
Sales Clerk:	Okay. Er... well, if you need any help...
Customer:	Yeah, I'm, I'm fine for now. Thank you.

Conversation 2

Customer:	Does it come with software?
Sales Clerk:	Yes, there are a few basic programs included.
Customer:	And, erm... how big is the memory?
Sales Clerk:	Pretty big. Unless you want to send lots of photos or video clips.
Customer:	Not really no. Just, er... you know, writing.
Sales Clerk:	Oh, no problems then. Er...so, what about a printer? We've got a nice range of...

Conversation 3

Sales Clerk:	Do you want to just take snaps or...?
Customer:	Actually, I'm thinking of starting a course. I'd like something a bit more advanced.
Sales Clerk:	Well, we have this one. The *ABX3000*. It's got a fast speed and comes with three types of lens.
Customer:	What kind of film does it take?
Sales Clerk:	I'm not sure. I'll just check.
Customer:	And can it take long exposures too?
Sales Clerk:	Er.. yeah, I think it.. Oh, Ron! Ron! Could you help this customer please?

Conversation 4

Customer:	Excuse me. Could you tell me a little bit about these two please?
Sales Clerk:	Sure. Erm... well, this one's the new one from *Sonic*. It's quite light, small—as you can see—you can store up to 300 numbers. You can choose from ten different melodies...
Customer:	Can it access the Internet?
Sales Clerk:	Yes, but it's a bit slow. Do you just want to do email?
Customer:	Well, I'd like to check information on the Web too. You know, concerts, restaurants maybe...
Sales Clerk:	Mm-hm. It can do that, but it takes a while to download. Now this one...
Customer:	That's the *Tote*, right?
Sales Clerk:	Yes ma'am. It does all the same things as the *Sonic* but it's much faster.
Customer:	It's a bit heavier though.
Sales Clerk:	And it stores fewer numbers. But the screen is bigger and clearer.
Customer:	How much does it cost?
Sales Clerk:	It's $185.95.
Customer:	Hmm. That's quite a lot.
Sales Clerk:	Yeah, but it does give you good Internet access so...
Customer:	How about the, er...
Sales Clerk:	The *Sonic*? It's much cheaper. $95.50. And it also comes with a carrying case.
Customer:	Is there a warranty?
Sales Clerk:	Of course ma'am. Both come with a one-year warranty. And if you pay a bit extra, we can increase that to three years.

Customer:	Okay, thanks. I'll think about it.
Sales Clerk:	No problem. Come back anytime.

Unit 4: Where's the toy department?

Conversation 1

Clerk:	Can I help you find something?
Customer:	Erm... yeah, I'm looking for a tie for my dad, er...
Clerk:	Try Menswear. It's on the fourth floor. Take that elevator, sir. Just behind you.
Customer:	Uh, where on the fourth floor?
Clerk:	Turn right out of the elevator, go past the leather goods and accessories, and go toward the front of the store. The ties are with the shirts. I think the ties are on sale this week. Have a look at the belts and wallets, too. They're also on sale.
Customer:	Right out of the elevator, past the accessories, near the shirts.
Clerk:	That's right.

Conversation 2

Customer:	Excuse me, I need to get a scarf for my mom.
Clerk:	Try Ladieswear, sir. It's, er... one floor up.
Customer:	One floor up. Right. And the scarves are...?
Clerk:	Ah yes. Er... when you get off the escalator, er... just walk straight ahead and you'll see the scarves on the right. Oh, by the way, we've got some very nice gloves just in. Er... your mother might like those too.
Customer:	Thanks. So that's up the escalator then straight, scarves and accessories are on the right.
Clerk:	That's right sir.

Conversation 3

Clerk:	What else can we do for you today?
Customer:	Well, I need a present for my nephew. He's just three.
Clerk:	Try the second floor, Children's and Toy department. There are a lot of cute picture books on the same floor if he likes picture books—have a look.
Customer:	Okay. Thanks. Er... where on the second floor exactly?
Clerk:	When you come out of the elevator, the toys will be on your left and the books on your right. The sporting goods and bikes are behind you.
Customer:	Toys on the left, books on the right, bikes in back. Thanks again.

Conversation 4

Clerk:	Is there anything else?
Customer:	Yeah, I want to get a CD for my brother.
Clerk:	They're downstairs in the basement. I suggest you take the stairs. It's faster than

the elevator.

Customer: Where in the basement?

Clerk: Just a moment, sir. Ah, yes. When you get to the bottom of the stairs, you'll be in the camera section. Turn left and go straight. You'll see the stereos and TVs. Go past the electronic goods, and the CDs and videos are on the right. Actually, we're having a sale on music videos and DVDs this month.

Customer: Okay. I'll take a look. Thanks. Um... left at the bottom of the stairs, past the TVs. CDs on the right.

Clerk: Right. You can't miss them.

Unit 5: Two tickets for tonight's show

Conversation 1

Recording: Thank you for calling *Concertmaster*, the only place to go for tickets to all major concerts and performances in the Metro area. We're sorry, but all our lines are busy at the moment. Please hold until someone can assist you. (music) Thank you for calling *Concertmaster*, the only place...

Caller: Oh, great.

Conversation 2

Ticket Agent: *Concert Choice*, may I help you?

Caller: Yes, I'd like two tickets for the Mississippi Blues Festival in April.

Ticket Agent: Could you please hold while I check on tickets?...

...Hello, sir? I'm afraid it's almost sold out. There are only a few seats left.

Caller: Uh oh. Where are they?

Ticket Agent: They're some on the first floor for $55 and some on the second floor for $45.

Caller: I see.

Ticket Agent: The seats on the first floor are beside the stage, and the seats on the second floor are on the side. Which would you prefer?

Caller: Sorry? Did you say beside the stage?

Ticket Agent: Yes, sir, that's right.

Caller: Great! I'll take them.

Conversation 3

Ticket Agent: *Concert Choice*, thank you for waiting. May I help you?

Caller: Yes, I'd like two tickets for the New York Philharmonic on May 18th. What's available in the orchestra section?

Ticket Agent: The orchestra section? Just a minute... uh, there are only a few seats left, but there are two together in that section. They're on the side. Would those be okay?

Caller: Excuse me, did you say the aisle?

Ticket Agent: No, the side.

Caller: Ah, the side. Are there any seats on the aisle?

Ticket Agent:	Let me check again. Yes, sir, there are, but they're much further back.
Caller:	How far back? Could you check?
Ticket Agent:	Let me see. Looks like they're about 40 rows back.
Caller:	Are they on the center aisle?
Ticket Agent:	No, they're on the left side.
Caller:	I see. Well, thanks for your time.

Conversation 4

Ticket Agent:	*Concert Choice*, thank you for waiting. How may I help you?
Caller:	I'd like tickets for the Jazz in the Park concert in June.
Ticket Agent:	How many tickets, sir?
Caller:	I need four.
Ticket Agent:	Four for Jazz in the Park. Will there be anything else?
Caller:	Yes, could you tell me where those seats are?
Ticket Agent:	Seating's not reserved, sir. You can sit anywhere. So if you want a good seat, you need to arrive early.
Caller:	Okay. Fine. How much are the tickets?
Ticket Agent:	$20 each, plus tax and service. For four tickets, that's $96. How would you like to pay?

Unit 5: Try It Out! Student A

Ask your partner questions and fill in your missing information.

Chicago Blues Revue
 Date: .... Time: .... Place: .... Ticket Price: ....

Jazz Under the Stars
 Date: .... Time: .... Place: .... Ticket Price: ....

Look at the information below. Answer any questions your partner asks.

Rock Monsters Festival
 Date: Oct 15 Time: 1-8 p.m. Place: City Arena Ticket Price: $30

Classical Afternoon
 Date: Sept 22 Time: 1-4 p.m. Place: Metro Hall Ticket Price: $15

Compare your work with your partner.

Unit 6: **What can I get you?**

Counter Staff:	Can I help you?
Customer:	Er.... Can I have the double cheeseburger combo, please?
Counter Staff:	And what would you like with that?
Customer:	Excuse me?
Counter Staff:	Would you like soup, salad or french fries?
Customer:	Er... french fries, please.
Counter Staff:	And to drink?
Customer:	Sorry?
Counter Staff:	What would you like to drink?
Customer:	Ah, drink. Do you have lemonade?
Counter Staff:	No. We have iced tea and cola.
Customer:	Oh. Okay. Iced tea.
Counter Staff:	Would you like that for here or to go?
Customer:	Sorry?
Counter Staff:	To eat in or to take out?
Customer:	Oh, to go, please. Er... could I have some extra napkins?
Counter Staff:	Your total is $3.56. Out of five, your change is $1.44. Napkins are over there on the counter. Next please.

Conversation 2

Counter Staff:	Welcome to *AstroBurger*. Can I take your order?
Customer:	Yeah, I'd like two kids' combos, a chickenburger combo and a deluxe burger combo, please.
Counter Staff:	Two kids' sets, a chickenburger set and the burger combo. What did you want to drink with that?
Customer:	What do you have?
Counter Staff:	Cola, diet cola, orange drink, lemon drink, grape drink, iced tea or coffee.
Customer:	Could you give me two small colas, and a medium grape drink and a medium coffee, please.
Counter Staff:	And did you want soup, salad or fries?
Customer:	Let me have four orders of fries, please.
Counter Staff:	Would you like anything else?
Customer:	No, that'll be it.
Counter Staff:	Is that for here or to go?
Customer:	For here, please.
Counter Staff:	Okay. Your total is $16.47. Out of $20. Your change is $3.53. Enjoy your meal.
Customer:	Thank you.

Conversation 3

Counter Staff:	May I take your order?
Customer:	Er… I'm sorry, could you give me a minute? Er… hm. Yes, could I have a chicken sandwich, a salad and a medium ginger ale please?
Counter Staff:	Did you want the set?
Customer:	The set?
Counter Staff:	The set's cheaper.
Customer:	Oh. Er… alright, then.
Counter Staff:	But we don't have ginger ale.
Customer:	Oh. What do you have?
Counter Staff:	Cola, diet cola, orange drink, lemon drink, grape drink, iced tea or coffee.
Customer:	Oh. Iced tea. With lemon?
Counter Staff:	No. No lemon sir.
Customer:	Oh, okay, erm…. yes the… cola, no diet-cola then please.
Counter Staff:	Okay, one chicken sandwich set, medium diet-coke, small salad. Thousand Island, French or Italian dressing?
Customer:	Er… Italian, please. Could I have some extra salt and pepper?
Counter Staff:	Help yourself. They're on the counter. Did you want that for here or to go?
Customer:	For here, please.
Counter Staff:	The total comes to $4.16. Out of $10. Your change is $5.84. Enjoy your meal.

Unit 5: Try It Out! Student B

Look at the information below. Answer any questions your partner asks.

Chicago Blues Revue
   Date: July 9   Time: 7-11 p.m.   Place: Blues Alley   Ticket Price: $25

Jazz Under the Stars
   Date: May 22   Time: 7-9:30 p.m.   Place: Central Park   Ticket Price: $20

Ask your partner questions and fill in your missing information.

Rock Monsters Festival
   Date: ....   Time: ....   Place: ....   Ticket Price: ....

Classical Afternoon
   Date: ....   Time: ....   Place: ....   Ticket Price: ....

Compare your work with your partner.

Unit 7: I'm terribly sorry, sir

Conversation 1

Mâitre D':	Good evening. Table for two?
Customers:	Ah yes.
Mâitre D':	Smoking or non smoking?
Customer:	Smoking please.
Mâitre D':	Okay. This way, please. Here we are. This is tonight's menu. Your server will be right with you... Ah.
Server:	Good evening. Are you ready to order?
Customer 1:	Er, could we have a few more minutes, please?
Server:	Of course. How about a drink while you decide?
Customer 1:	Ah. Please. Yes, um. I'll have a glass of red wine, and um...
Customer 2:	Oh, er.. a glass of white wine for me.
Server:	Of course. I'll be right back.
Customer 1:	Well, the service is rather quick here...
Customer 2:	Sure is.
Customer 2:	...it's good...
Server:	Here you are, one glass of red and one glass of white wine.
Customer 2:	Mine is the white, his the red.
Server.	Of course, I'm sorry about that. Would you like to order now?
Customer 1:	Ah, yes. I'm afraid this wine is, eh, is cold. Ah, red wine shouldn't really be chilled. It's um...
Server:	I'm very sorry about that (Um). The wine waiter's off sick today. I suppose (Ah yes) someone must have chilled it by mistake. (Right) I'll change it for you...
Customer 1:	Yes if you could.

Conversation 2

Customer 1:	And so what I'm saying is we need to find a company that can deliver on time...
Server:	Sorry to keep you waiting. It's always like this at lunch. Um... are you ready to order?
Customer 1:	Yeah, I'd like the salad with the oil and vinegar dressing, and the grilled chicken.
Customer 2:	And I'll have the same salad, but the pasta.
Customer 1:	And a bottle of water, please.
Customer 2:	And could you also bring me another fork? This one's a bit...
Server:	I'm sorry, of course.
Customer 2:	So yeah, I know what you mean. If the supplier can't guarantee delivery, then we've got to find someone who can.
Server:	Your salads. Sir? Ma'am? And a bottle of white wine.
Customer 1:	I'm sorry, but I asked for a bottle of water.
Server:	Oh, I do apologize ma'am. Sorry, the wine's for Table Six behind you. I'll be back with your water in just a second.
Customer 1:	And the fork, please?

Server: Be right with you ma'am.

Customer 2:   Talk about delivery problems!

Conversation 3

Child: Eww!

Mother: What's wrong?

Child: It's cold, mom. Can you get the waitress?

Mother: Oh, Let me see. It's not that cold. Eat your dinner.

Child: It is. It's cold!

Mother: Alright. George, can you…?

Father: Yeah, alright darling. Er… excuse me?

Server: Yes?

Father: I'm afraid this is cold. Could you bring us another one?

Server: Oh, I'm very sorry. I'll get you another one right away.

Mother: Here, have some of mine while we're waiting.

Child: I don't like that. What's taking so long?

Father: Excuse me?

Server: Yes?

Father: Er… I'm afraid we're still waiting for my daughter's food. And about my son's entrée…

Server: It's coming right now sir. I'm very sorry.

Child: I'm hungry!

Server:: Here you go young lady. And, er… we're so sorry about all the trouble. How about an ice cream for dessert?

Child: Ice cream.

Server: Our treat of course.

Father: Oh. That, that's very kind. Thank you.

Unit 8: Now here's the weather

Anchor: Now, let's go over to the weather center and Peter Stevens. Peter?

Weatherman: Thanks, Salim. So, looking at tomorrow's forecast for the world's major regions. Let's begin in Asia. As you can see, a cold front's moving towards East Asia and this will probably bring bad weather early this week. For the rest of the week it's likely to be cloudy, with some rain. It could be windy this week as well. Temperatures will probably range from a low of 16 to 18 in the evenings to daytime highs of between 25 to 26 degrees.

Moving east, the Pacific is going to have thunderstorms. Some of these thunderstorms could be very heavy, and it's going to be very windy in some places. The seven-day forecast for the Pacific area is rain, rain and more rain, with temperatures in the 20's.

Turning now to the Middle East, the weather in this region will be clear, dry and very hot, temperatures in the low-to-mid-30's. And it's going to stay that way all week. There's not much chance of rain either.

Over to Northern Africa and this week will be sunny and clear. Look for highs of 27, 28 and lows of around 22. Quite pleasant in fact. As with the Middle East, there's not much chance of rain though you might see the odd shower here and there.

Southern Africa. Sunny skies and clear all this week. Dry everywhere and it's going to be very hot this week. Lows probably around 30 reaching highs of 34 or even 35 degrees centigrade. So if you're going to be outside a lot, remember to put on your sun block.

Last but not least Europe this week, much of the south is going to be bright and sunny, but it might also be a bit windy at times. Temperatures are likely to be in the mid-20's.

Northern Europe will have clear skies but some fairly cool weather. Some areas, France, Germany for example, may be a little chilly early in the morning. Temperatures will probably be between 13 and 17 degrees.

That's your world weather for the week. Now, back to Salim.

Anchor: Thanks Peter. Sport now, and the finals of the....

Unit 9: Can I speak to Bill, please?

Conversation 1

Tom:	Hi, Barbara, this is Tom. Can I speak to Jim, please?
Barbara:	Oh, hi, Tom. I'm sorry, you've just missed him.
Tom:	Oh. Er, could you ask him to give me a call when he gets in? Um, it's about our tennis match. I don't remember what time we're meeting.
Barbara:	Sure. Give me your number and I'll have him call you back when he gets in.
Tom:	Okay, yeah. Erm... I'll give you my cell number. Er... it's er... 555-4544-0971.
Barbara:	555-4544-0971?
Tom:	That's right, yeah.
Barbara:	Okay. I'll tell him [to] call you.
Tom:	Thanks a lot. Bye.
Barbara:	Bye.

Conversation 2

Receptionist:	Good morning, *Digital Systems*. May I help you?
Dan Harris:	Hello, yes. This is Dan Harris from *Megatronics*. Is Mark Whitman there, please?

Receptionist:	I'm sorry, sir, I didn't catch your name.
Dan Harris:	Harris. I need to speak to Mark Whitman about our appointment this afternoon.
Receptionist:	Of course Mr. Harris, I'll see if he's in. Please hold. Thank you for waiting. I'm afraid Mr. Whitman's in a meeting.
Dan Harris:	I see. Something's come up and I need to reschedule our appointment. Okay. I'll call him back later. Do you know how long he'll be tied up?

Conversation 3

Grant Richards:	Hi, this is Grant Richards, could I speak to Rachael, please?
Friend:	Rachel? I'll see if she's in. Hello? Sorry, I thought she was here, but....
Grant Richards:	Could I leave a message? It's about work.
Friend:	Sure, just let me get a pencil...go ahead.
Grant Richards:	Could you ask her to call Grant at 523-0982, please?
Friend:	Okay.
Grant Richards:	I need to know if she can work this Saturday.
Friend:	Sure, I'll give her the message.
Grant Richards:	Thanks very much. Bye-bye.
Friend:	Bye.

Conversation 4

Allen:	Hello?
Dave:	Allen, this is Dave. Mom said you called.
Allen:	Yeah. What are you doing today?
Dave:	I don't know, why?
Allen:	Well I've got tickets to the ball game this afternoon.
Dave:	Wow! Where did you get them?
Allen:	Don't ask! You want to come?
Dave:	You kidding? Yeah sure I want to come. Thanks.
Allen:	Okay, we're all going to meet at the stadium, at the entrance to the . . . .

Unit 10: First day on the job

Conversation 1

Mr. Banks:	Andrea, do you have a minute?
Andrea Garcia:	Of course, Mr. Banks, come in.
Mr. Banks:	Andrea, I'd like you to meet Paul Smothers. He'll will be working with us this summer. Paul, let me introduce you to Andrea Garcia, our Features Editor. She'll be your supervisor. Andrea, can you introduce Paul to the staff this morning?
Andrea Garcia:	Certainly Mr. Banks.
Paul Smothers:	Thank you, Mr. Banks.
Andrea Garcia:	Nice to meet you, Paul. Welcome to *Great Lakes Magazine*.

Paul Smothers: Thank you very much. I'm pleased to meet you. I've read some of your articles. You're from Madison, aren't you?

Andrea Garcia: That's right. How about yourself?

Paul Smothers: Me, too.

Andrea Garcia: Oh, really? So, Paul, there are some other people you'll need to meet. Just let me save this file and I'll introduce you....there. Ready?

Paul Smothers: Sure.

Conversation 2

Andrea Garcia: Elaine, have you met Paul Smothers? Paul, this is Elaine Lincoln, our Sales Manager.

Paul Smothers: I'm pleased to meet you, Ms. Lincoln.

Elaine Lincoln: Nice to meet you Paul. Please call me Elaine. So, you're from *Great Lakes State*?

Paul Smothers: That's right. You were at school there, right?

Elaine Lincoln: You've done your homework, Paul. Yes, I went to college there. Actually, I had a job selling advertising for the school paper.

Paul Smothers: Really! I was on the school paper...

Elaine Lincoln: Anyway, It was nice to meet you. Stop by any time if you want to talk.

Paul Smothers: Thanks very much. I will.

Conversation 3

Andrea Garcia: Hi, Cindi. You busy?

Cindi Morgan: Not really. Just a second. There.

Andrea Garcia: Cindi, this is Paul. Paul, do you know Cindi Morgan, our secretary?

Paul Smothers: I don't think so. Nice to meet you.

Cindi Morgan: You too, Paul. You know, you look kind of familiar.

Paul Smothers: Really?

Cindi Morgan: You're from Madison, aren't you?

Paul Smothers: Yeah, I grew up there.

Cindi Morgan: Do you know Tim Morgan?

Paul Smothers: Tim? Sure I just saw him last week.

Cindi Morgan: Tim's my little brother.

Paul Smothers: Oh! It's a small world. So you went to *Stephens*, too?

Unit 11: I'm interested in taking a course

Receptionist: Good morning, *Hudson College*. Er... how may I help you?

Raoul Martinez: Yes, my name is Raoul Martinez. I'm calling from Panama. I would like some information about your English courses.

Receptionist: Yes, of course. Ah, what would you like to know?

Raoul Martinez: Yeah, I saw your ad in the Gazette for intensive English courses. Er, what are the dates for Advanced Business English course please?

Receptionist: That course runs from June 24th until August 7th.

Raoul Martinez: June 24 'til August 7. Right. And how much does it cost?

Receptionist: Tuition is $1200, but that doesn't include room and board.

Raoul Martinez: $1200 plus living expenses.

Receptionist: That's right.

Raoul Martinez: And.., how many hours a day does it meet?

Receptionist: Advanced Business English? Er… just a second. Er, yes. It meets 15 hours a week. Er… that means you'll need a student visa. Ah, we will send you the forms you need for that when we get your deposit.

Raoul Martinez: I see. They're morning classes I suppose?

Receptionist: Actually, the advanced course is in the afternoon, from 1:30 to 4:30.

Raoul Martinez: 1:30 to 4:30. And five days a week, right?

Receptionist: Yes sir. Monday to Friday, afternoons.

Raoul Martinez: I see. And is there a lot of homework?

Receptionist: Well, it really depends on the instructor...

Unit 11: Try It Out! Student A

Ask questions and fill in the information about the *Painting*, *Aerobics* and *Swimming* classes.

Course:	Day	Time	Length	Cost	Bring
Painting					
Aerobics					
Swimming					

Answer your partner's questions about the *Oriental Cooking*, *Photography* and *Computer Skills* classes.

Course:	Day	Time	Length	Cost	Bring
Oriental Cooking	Mon	6-7:30 p.m.	8 weeks	$50	apron
Photography	Wed	7-9 p.m.	12 weeks	$60	camera, film
Computer Skills	Thu	7-8:30 p.m.	6 weeks	$35	nothing

Check your work.

Raoul Martinez: Hm. And about how many students are there per class?

Receptionist: No more than 12, but usually only seven or eight.

Raoul Martinez: That's pretty small, good. Oh, can language students use the school facilities?

Receptionist: Oh, of course. You can use the library, gym, pool, student center. Er... Mr. Martinez, this call must be costing you a lot. Why don't I send you one of our brochures and you can find out more about us and er... then if you like...

Raoul Martinez: Yes, that would be great. And could you please send me an application form too?

Unit 12: What time do we arrive?

Part One

Travel Agent: Good morning, may I help you?

Customer: I'd like to make a reservation for four from Hong Kong to San Francisco.

Travel Agent: I'm sorry, what's your destination?

Customer: Hm, San Francisco.

Travel Agent: And the departure date?

Customer: August 3rd.

Travel Agent: And what's the return date?

Customer: The 24th.

Travel Agent: And your last name please?

Customer: Bicksby.

Travel Agent: Bigsby.

Customer: No not Bigsby. It's Bicksby. B-I-C-K-S-B-Y.

Travel Agent: Mrs. Bicksby.

Customer: That's it.

Part Two

Travel Agent: I'm afraid all the flights on the 24th are full. Could you return a day earlier or later?

Customer: Hm... Let me think, hang on.. er ... The 23rd. That's a Saturday, isn't it?

Travel Agent: That's right.

Customer: Okay, the 23rd's fine.

Travel Agent: Okay, let me just check on that, then... right... There are only a few seats left...

Customer: As I said, I need four seats.

Travel Agent: I'm sorry, did you say four seats?

Customer: Yes, I said four seats. Together. For a family of four.

Travel Agent: I'm sorry, I thought you said a reservation for Hong Kong from San Francisco. I'm sorry. Let me just have another look. I'm sure we can find something for you.

Part Three

Travel Agent: Okay, we're all set.

Customer: Great.

Travel Agent: Your flight number on August 3rd is UA796 from Hong Kong to San Francisco. You depart Hong Kong at 11:30 a.m., arrive in San Francisco the same day at 8:15 a.m. local time.

Customer: 8:15 a.m. okay.

Travel Agent: Now, the return flight you've got two choices (Hmm). The first is UA797 which departs San Francisco at 5:30 a.m. on August 23rd, and arrives in Hong Kong at 12:30 p.m., August 24th. That's the following day.

Customer: Okay, okay.

Travel Agent: Or, you can take UA763, which leaves San Francisco at 7:30 a.m., stops in Tokyo at 10:30 a.m. August 24, departs at 5:30 p.m. and arrives in Hong Kong at 10:30 p.m. on the 24th.

Customer: Wow, that's a long flight.

Travel Agent: Yes ma'am, it is. But it's a lot cheaper because of the stopover.

Unit 11: Try It Out! Student B

Answer your partner's questions about the *Painting*, *Aerobics* and *Swimming* classes.

Course:	Day	Time	Length	Cost	Bring
Painting	Sat	10 a.m.-1 p.m.	12 weeks	$60	paint & brushes
Aerobics	Sat	3-5 p.m.	8 weeks	$50	towel
Swimming	Tue-Thu	4-5:30 p.m.	6 weeks	$45	goggles, towel, cap

Ask questions and fill in the information about the *Oriental Cooking*, *Photography* and *Computer Skills* classes.

Course:	Day	Time	Length	Cost	Bring
Oriental Cooking					
Photography					
Computer Skills					

Check your work.

Customer:	Hmm, okay. Ah, let me just confirm that. August 3rd at 11:30 a.m. UA796 from Hong Kong to San Francisco....
Travel Agent:	Right.
Customer:	...and August 23rd at 5:30 a.m. UA797 from San Francisco arriving in Hong Kong the next day at er, 12:30 p.m.
Travel Agent:	Right.
Customer:	Or UA763 leaving San Francisco at 7:30 a.m. on the 23rd. That stops in Tokyo for seven hours, and we get into Hong Kong at 10:30 p.m. the next day. How much cheaper is this flight?
Travel Agent:	Er... it's quite a bit less, I think. Let me just check that for you.

Unit 13: Rules of the house

Mrs. Weiss:	Mr. Isaiah?
Mr. Isaiah:	Er... Isaiah, yes. Er... Mrs. Weiss?
Mrs. Weiss:	Come in then. You'll be up at the university?
Mr. Isaiah:	Er... yes. I'm going to be teaching a course in...
Mrs. Weiss:	Well, come on then. Right. Here's the living room, (Ah) next to the kitchen as you can see (Yes... yes). There's the TV. Oh, please keep the volume down, and turn it off if no one's watching (Right). And if you could try to keep this room neat... it's for everyone so...
Mr. Isaiah:	Yes, o-of course. And, er... ah! I see there's a, a phone's there. Is it okay to, to call home?
Mrs. Weiss:	Yes, but you'll have to call collect and keep calls short, (Right) a couple of minutes or so (I see). Or use the pay phone at the end of the road (Oh). Unless there's an emergency or something, then...
Mr. Isaiah:	Okay. Right, I see. And, er... is it okay to use the phone anytime? Ah there's a, a time difference, so if I have to call late at night or something...
Mrs. Weiss:	That's fine, but late at night you should talk quietly.
Mr. Isaiah:	Yes, of course.
Mrs. Weiss:	Well, if that's okay then, er... the kitchen's just here (Right). Be very careful using the stove, and turn it off just as soon as you finish cooking (Okay, yeah). Remember to wash up and when you're done don't leave the dishes out, (The dishes out, um, yes) put them away here in this cupboard. And er... the fridge is over here (Right). Please keep your food in here, on the middle shelf.
Mr. Isaiah:	The, the middle shelf, right thanks. Um, um, I can take meals up to my room, I presume?
Mrs. Weiss:	Uh , well no, (No...no...oh...oh) I'd rather you didn't do that, no.
Mr. Isaiah:	Oh, um, well do, do you mind if I take food into the the living room? Um. Is it okay to eat while watching TV or something?
Mrs. Weiss:	No, I'm sorry... No. Please eat in the kitchen...

Mr. Isaiah:	Ah yes, uh, okay.....
Mrs. Weiss:	So, I'll show you the bathroom, then. It's right beside your room, quite convenient really. (Hmm, yes) Everyone shares, so make sure you knock. (You knock, right) Now, please don't stay in the shower for more than five minutes, and you have to buy your own soap and shampoo and towels.
Mr. Isaiah:	Towels? I, I didn't hear...
Mrs. Weiss:	Please don't leave your things in here when you've finished, and try not to waste the water.
Mr. Isaiah:	Ah, yeah, er about the towels, could I borrow...
Mrs. Weiss:	And here is your room, just next door (Right). Now, I should have told you before, but please be sure to turn out the lights when you go out (Right, yeah), and always lock your door when you leave. Just in case. (Jus-just in case) And sorry but there's no smoking or eating in the bedrooms.
Mr. Isaiah:	Ah, a... Actually, I don't smoke so ah...
Mrs. Weiss:	Now this is my room, across the hall. (Right) I'm usually in here. (Ah, oh good) If the door is closed, please knock. (Knock, yes) Now, do you have any questions?
Mr. Isaiah:	Yeah well yes. How about friends or colleagues? Um, do you mind if I invite people over?
Mrs. Weiss:	No (No), of course not (That's great), but please don't invite anyone into your room (Ah). It's safer that way (Right). You can invite friends to watch TV or do (I see) something downstairs.
Mr. Isaiah:	O... Okay, I understand. And there aren't any chores we need to do around the house or anything? Other...
Mrs. Weiss:	Well, you don't have to do anything special like vacuuming, (Ah, ok good) but you should keep your room neat (Neat, yep), tidy up the living room (Yes), keep the kitchen clean (Clean), you know (Yeah), if everyone does just a little bit (Ah, yes) then things will be better (Right) for everyone.
Mr. Isaiah:	Yes, er, a... actually Mrs. Weiss. I think there must have been some sort of mistake.

Unit 12: Practice! Student A

Look at the information in the timetable below. Student B has a similar timetable *with some differences*. Ask Student B questions. Find at least seven differences in your flight schedules.

Date	Flight	Airline	From	To	Departure	Arrival
Sept. 30	RA07	Raven Air	Vancouver	Chicago	08:35	15:20
Oct. 4	EF131	Easyflight	Chicago	Denver	09:35	11:00
Oct. 4	RA30	Raven Air	Denver	Vancouver	13:50	15:35

Unit 14: Haven't you changed

Suzanne:	Amelia?
Amelia:	Suzanne? How are you? Wow, you look great!
Suzanne:	Thanks. You too. How have you been?
Amelia:	Not bad. I almost didn't recognize you. You've really changed.
Suzanne:	Yeah, it's my new look.
Amelia:	It really suits you. What did you do?
Suzanne:	Well, you know, I used to be so overweight. One day I just looked in the mirror and decided to go on a diet. Then I started aerobics, and I've been swimming. So far I've lost about six kilos.
Amelia:	Good for you... I ought to do the same.
Suzanne:	You don't need to. You've always been thin.
Amelia:	Your hair looks different, too.
Suzanne:	I found a great stylist. Remember how my hair used to be long and straight, and just kind of... brown? Well, I had it cut, then I got a perm, and finally I had it colored, just in a few places.
Amelia:	The color's lighter than it was. It looks great with your skin.
Suzanne:	It makes my face look thinner. My face used to look so round.
Amelia:	And your eyes...what did you....
Suzanne:	Colored contacts. You remember I used to wear glasses..
Amelia:	Yeah.
Suzanne:	...but these contacts were just the perfect color. I just love them. But enough about me. Look at you. You're looking good.
Amelia:	Thanks. I haven't changed much since high school, really.
Suzanne:	No, you haven't. And you look so healthy. Your skin tone is so good, and it seems like you're taller or something.
Amelia:	Actually I've gained a little weight. I've been exercising a couple of times a week for a while now... I'm careful about what I eat. Not a diet, but health food. I jog a lot. I feel good. You know, in high school I was always the short skinny girl with the short curly hair. I needed a change, so I let my hair grow long, so it would look thicker. Then I started working out, and...I feel better about myself.
Suzanne:	And you look great. Your makeup....
Amelia:	I didn't use to wear much makeup when I was in school, but now I've started wearing a little. And I've been getting a lot of sun, too. I used to be so pale, but now with the tan.
Suzanne:	You look... I don't know... stronger. Healthy.

Unit 15: Going away for the summer?

Conversation 1

Judy: Hey, Eric. So, what are you doing over the summer? Any plans?

Eric: I don't know really. Um, I'd kind of like to travel, you know, maybe go somewhere and get away from it all for a while.

Judy: Know what you mean, just relax, take it easy.

Eric: But I'm going to have to stay here. I'll probably get a part-time job and maybe just hang out, surf the web.

Judy: That sounds a bit grim.

Eric: Yeah, well... I might go somewhere later if I can save some money, but I doubt I'll be able to. How about you Judy? Are you going to see your folks?

Judy: Yeah, I'm going to drive down this weekend.

Eric: Should be fun. They've got a beach house, right?

Judy: Yeah, so I'm going to take it easy, go to the beach, you know, just do nothing. But I know my parents are going to tell me to find a job.

Eric: Know what Judy? They sound like mine.

Judy: Yeah, so I'll probably have to, but maybe I'll be able to work at night, a coffee shop or something.

Eric: Hm. So, have a good vacation, yeah? I'll see you after the break.

Judy: Thanks, you, too. Have a good break.

Conversation 2

Ian: So, what are you going to do over the holidays, Chrissy? Are you going anywhere?

Chrissy: You know what Ian? I really wanted to go somewhere, you know, swim, get a tan. But I doubt we'll be able to now. We're going to be here over the break.

Ian: How come?

Chrissy: Justin's got to work. Just yesterday, his boss calls him in and tells him he has to work. Then he found out the reason is his boss is going on vacation, so Justin's got to cover for him.

Ian: Oh, that's too bad.

Chrissy: Yeah, well. So anyway, I'm going find something to do with the kids while he's at work. We might go to the beach or something when his boss gets back. How about you, Ian? What are you guys up to?

Ian: We're not going to do anything special either. We may just drive up to the mountains and spend a few days there. The kids can play, and we can just read or hike. We'll probably end up just watching TV.

Listening Clinic 2

1.   I've got to work.

2.   What do you have to do today?

3.   Are you going to go home?

4.   I don't want to go this weekend.

5.   Would you please turn that down?

6.   Could you tell me tomorrow?

Look at the information in the timetable below. Student A has a similar timetable *with some differences*. Ask Student A questions. Find at least seven differences in your flight schedules.

Date	Flight	Airline	From	To	Departure	Arrival
Sept. 30	RA70	Raven Air	Seattle	Chicago	08:35	14:45
Oct. 5	EF131	Easyflight	Chicago	Denver	09:35	11:00
Oct. 5	EF262	Easyflight	Denver	Seattle	13:50	15:30

Word Lists

Unit 1: It's famous for soccer

romantic	related to love
temple	a building where people worship nature or god(s)
costume	clothes worn in a particular place or for a special occassion
....	a place many travelers want to see
....	to say something is good
....	to say what you think someone should do
spicy	....
pyramid	....
prompt (n)	....
....	....
....	....
....	....

Unit 2: How have you been?

to get promoted	to be given a higher position job
how's it going?	a casual expression which means *how are you?*
I can't complain	an expression which means *things are good*
....	a time you agree to meet someone
....	someone you have known for a long time
....	an expression you use when you see someone you have not seen for a long time
congratulations	....
what's up?	....

to get together ....

....

....

....

Unit 3: Can I help you ma'am?

to access	*in computing*, to open a file, enter the Internet or enter a website
warranty	a promise from a company to fix a product if it does not work
accessories	equipment that is in addition to the basics
....	an instrument that shows you where you are driving
....	a quickly taken picture
....	the amount of light that enters a camera when you take a picture
to come with	....
to take a while	....
to store	....
....	....
....	....
....	....

Unit 4: Where's the toy department?

counter (n)	a flat surface used to serve customers
to go past	to go beyond where something is
department	a section in a store or company
....	to give a possible solution to a problem
....	an expression which means something is *easy to see*
....	to replace something with another thing

to take a look	....
bargain	....
bin	....
....	....
....	....
....	....

Unit 5: Two tickets for tonight's show

service	service charge
expiry date	after this date something can no longer be used
hard to satisfy	not easily pleased
....	a place you buy tickets
....	a showing of a play or dance or other entertainment
....	an expression which means *the telephone is being used*
to check on	....
to sell out	....
available	....
....	....
....	....
....	....

Unit 6: What can I get you?

diet (adj)	a word you use to describe food or drink that does not make you fat
that'll be	an expression you use when you say how much something costs
here you are	an expression you use when you give somebody something

	food you do not have to wait for
....	an expression you use when you make an order
....	a small dish you eat with a main dish
extra	....
combo	....
to go	....
....	....
....	....
....	....

Unit 7: I'm terribly sorry, sir

to chill	to make something cool
entrée	the main part of a meal
my treat	an expression you use when you buy someone something
....	a person who brings you food in a restaurant
....	to eat in a restaurant
....	not polite
complain	....
supplier	....
what's taking so long?	....
....	....
....	....
....	....

Unit 8: Now here's the weather

retired	a word you use to describe a person who is no longer working
shower	a short rainfall
chilly	a little cold
....	an area of the world or of a country
....	a guess about what will happen in the future
....	giving a nice feeling
thunderstorm	....
you might see the odd...	....
symbol	....
....	....
....	....
....	....

Unit 9: Can I speak to Bill, please?

to be tied up	to be busy with one thing so you cannot do another
are you kidding?	an expression you use to show surprise
go ahead	an expression which means *I don't mind if you do this*
....	to change the time or date of a meeting or event
....	to write down information from one person to give to another person
....	to use a telephone
something came up	....
to miss someone	....
don't ask	....
....	....

....

....

Unit 10: First day on the job

reserved	not showing emotion
easy stuff	small jobs that are not difficult to do
to grow up	to become an adult
....	someone who is in charge of a group of people
....	a piece of writing in a newspaper or magazine
....	to visit for a short time
file	....
staff member	....
you look familiar	....
....	....
....	....
....	....

Unit 11: I'm interested in taking a course

living expenses	money needed for daily life
facility	buildings or equipment you use for a special purpose
application form	a paper you fill in to enter a course or organization
....	glasses to protect the eyes
....	needing much effort and attention
....	arranging things in a photograph in a nice way
include	....
deposit (n)	....

it depends (on...) ....

....

....

....

Unit 12: What time do we arrive?

hang on	a casual expression which means *wait*
we're all set	an expression which means *we are ready*
departure date	the date you are leaving for someplace
....	a place you are going
....	the day, month and year you are born
....	to stop something that was planned
baggage claim	....
let's see what we can do	....
stopover	....
....	....
....	....
....	....

Unit 13: Rules of the house

I'd rather you didn't	a polite expression which means *don't do something*
to presume	to think something is true because it is likely
inspector	a person whose job is to check that things are in order
....	a job you do not like to do but have to do
....	easy to use because of the time or the place

	a short word for refrigerator
to knock	....
to waste	....
annoyed	....
....	....
....	....
....	....

Unit 14: Haven't you changed

good for you	an expression you use when you think someone did something well
tone	color
relative	a member of your extended family
....	skin made darker by the sun
....	to know who someone is when you see them
....	to become less heavy
for one's age	....
used to be	....
used to do something	....
....	....
....	....
....	....

Unit 15: Going away for the summer?

how come?	a casual expression which means *why?*
to take it easy	to relax, to go slowly
break (n)	a time of rest

....   a casual word which means *parents*

....   person in charge

....   rich

to get away from it all   ....

to hang out   ....

to cover for somebody   ....

....

....

....

Audio CD Tracks for Exercises